EMIRATI DEFENCE EVOLUTION

Emirati Defence Evolution

FROM IMPORTS TO AUTONOMY

GEW Intelligence Unit

Hichem Karoui (Ed.)

Global East-West (London)

Contents

Foreword   1

    I Introduction   5

    II Historical Context   18

A. Evolution of the UAE's Defence Industry   23

B. Previous Dependence on Foreign Defence
Imports   29

C. Catalysts for Change   33

    III The Motivations Behind Defence Emiratisation   38

A. Economic Factors   41

B. Technological Ambitions   45

C. Geopolitical Considerations   49

D. Regional Security Concerns   53

    IV National Security Implications   56

A. Reduced Dependencies on Foreign Suppliers 61

B. Enhancing Strategic Autonomy   **65**

C. Resilience to Geopolitical Shifts   **69**

    V Impact on National Defence Strategies   72

A. Reconfiguration of Defence Policies   **77**

B. Adaptation to Changing Geopolitical Dynamics   **83**

C. Alignment with National Security Objectives   **95**

    VI Evolution of Military Doctrines   99

A. Integration of Local Technologies   **103**

B. Adaptation to Localised Defence Capabilities   **109**

C. Implications for Regional Military Cooperation   **113**

    VII Performance of the National Armed Forces   116

A. Enhanced Capabilities through Emiratisation   121

B. Challenges and Opportunities   125

C. Comparative Analysis with Previous Import-Dependant Models   129

VIII   National Defence Budgets   134

A. Economic Impacts of Defence Emiratisation   139

B. Allocation of Resources   145

IX   Implications for the National Economy   153

A. Economic Diversification through Defence Emiratisation   161

B. Job Creation and Skill Development   167

C. Broader Economic Impacts   171

X   Geopolitical Ramifications for the Gulf Region   175

A. Recalibration of Alliances in Defence Emiratisation   179

B. Power Dynamics in the Gulf   183

C. Influence on International Relations   187

XI Conclusion   190

A. Summary of Findings   195

B. Future Prospects and Recommendations   199

References For Further Reading   204

Foreword

Current State of the UAE's Domestic Defence Industry

The United Arab Emirates (UAE) has been working towards establishing a robust local defence industry to reduce its reliance on imports and become a significant player in the global defence market. This initiative is part of a broader strategy to diversify its economy from oil dependency and achieve greater strategic autonomy. The UAE's efforts in this direction have been multifaceted, involving the development of local defence manufacturing capabilities, strategic partnerships, and significant investments in research and development.

DEVELOPMENT AND EXPANSION

The UAE's defence industry has grown considerably over the past decade, focusing on developing armoured vehicles, aerospace, naval vessels, and advanced weaponry capabilities. Companies like EDGE Group, a conglomerate of over 25 integrated defence entities, have been at the forefront of this push, working on enhancing the UAE's defence manufacturing capabilities. EDGE Group, in particular, has been instrumental in consolidating the UAE's defence industry, fostering innovation, and pursuing strategic international partnerships to bolster its technological capabilities and market reach.

STRATEGIC PARTNERSHIPS AND INTERNATIONAL COOPERATION

The UAE has actively sought partnerships with international defence firms and governments to accelerate the development of its indigenous defence industry. These partnerships often involve technology transfer agreements, joint ventures, and collaborative research and development projects. For instance, the UAE has signed framework agreements with Turkey to strengthen defence industry ties, involving collaborations between Emirati conglomerate Edge Group and several Turkish defence companies. Such arrangements enhance the UAE's defence manufacturing capabilities and open opportunities for Emirati defence products in new markets.

FOCUS ON ADVANCED TECHNOLOGIES

The UAE's defence industry strategy strongly emphasises developing advanced technologies, including unmanned aerial systems (UAS), missile systems, and cyber defence capabilities. The development of the indigenous Reach-S UAS by the Emirati defence firm Edge Group, set to begin production in 2024, exemplifies the UAE's ambition to lead in cutting-edge defence technologies. Additionally, the UAE's investments in foreign defence firms and its efforts to integrate locally developed munitions onto international platforms indicate a strategic approach to building a competitive edge in the global defence market.

CHALLENGES AND FUTURE OUTLOOK

Challenges remain while the UAE has significantly progressed in developing its indigenous defence industry. These include the high costs associated with defence manufacturing, the need for skilled labour, and the complexities of competing in a market dominated by established global players.

However, the UAE's strategic investments, focus on niche technologies, and efforts to foster international partnerships position it well to overcome these challenges and achieve its long-term objectives.

This book explains the importance of the Defence Emiratisation project. This volume (another brick in the wall of the collection "The Gulf") delves into the United Arab Emirates (UAE) journey towards defence control, exploring its historical context, motivations, national security implications, impact on defence strategies, the evolution of military doctrines, performance of the national armed forces, national defence budgets, consequences for the national economy, and the geopolitical ramifications for the Gulf region. It emphasises the UAE's transition from heavy reliance on foreign defence imports to pursuing a self-sustaining defence industry.

Purpose and Scope of the Book

- The book aims to comprehensively analyse defence Emiratisation, examining its motivations, implications, and impact from various perspectives.

- It delves into national security implications, the evolution of military doctrines, and the performance evaluation of the national armed forces after implementing defence Emiratisation measures.

- The motivations for this national defence project encompass economic factors, technological ambitions, geopolitical considerations, and regional security concerns, all of which need to be considered and analysed.

1. What are the key motivations behind the UAE's pursuit of defence control?

2. How does defence control contribute to the UAE's national security objectives and economic diversification goals?

3. What are the implications of the UAE's pursuit of defence control for the broader geopolitical context and regional security dynamics?

These are a few questions among the many this volume of the collection "The Gulf" addresses.

As we see it, the UAE's domestic defence industry is on a rapid growth and diversification trajectory, driven by strategic investments, international partnerships, and a focus on advanced technologies. As the industry continues to evolve, the UAE is poised to meet its national defence needs more independently and become a significant exporter of defence products and technologies on the global stage.

Hichem Karoui, Research Director and Editor.

I

Introduction

Throughout history, defence has played a critical role in the survival and stability of nations. In today's complex geopolitical landscape, the United Arab Emirates (UAE) recognises the importance of building a solid local defence industry. This book aims to examine the significance of defence Emiratisation in the UAE, exploring its historical context, motivations, national security implications, impact on defence strategies, the evolution of military doctrines, the performance of the national armed forces, national defence budgets, consequences for the national economy, and the geopolitical ramifications for the Gulf region.

The UAE's journey towards defence Emiratisation is rooted in its past reliance on foreign defence imports. For years, the country heavily depended on external sources to meet its defence needs, which had implications for its strategic autonomy and national security. The UAE's experience during the Gulf War in 1990-1991 shaped its attitude towards self-reliance. The dependency on foreign allies for military intervention highlighted the vulnerability of the nation's defence capabilities. This realisation sparked the UAE's resolve to strengthen its defence industry and move towards Emiratisation.

However, recent shifts in global dynamics, technological advancements, and regional security concerns have catalysed accelerated change. The UAE has recognised the need to reduce its dependence on foreign suppliers and develop an autonomous defence industry catering to its unique requirements. This pursuit of defence Emiratisation aligns with the country's broader economic diversification goals as outlined in the UAE Vision 2021 and the UAE Centennial 2071. By fostering technological innovation, research and development, and local partnerships, the UAE aims to build a robust defence industry capable of catering to its specific defence needs, creating employment opportunities and driving economic growth.

The significance of defence Emiratisation in the UAE extends beyond enhancing national security and achieving economic diversification. It also has profound implications for defence strategies and military doctrines. The UAE can tailor its defence strategies to suit its unique geopolitical challenges by developing local defence capabilities. This allows for a more nuanced approach to regional security concerns, as the UAE's defence industry can be closely integrated with its defence planning and decision-making processes. Adapting and responding swiftly to changing threats and security dynamics is crucial for maintaining national sovereignty and ensuring the security of the UAE and its interests.

Moreover, defence Emiratisation impacts the performance of the national armed forces. By leveraging locally developed technologies and equipment, the UAE's armed forces can achieve higher interoperability, operational readiness, and combat effectiveness. Local defence capabilities allow for greater flexibility and agility in adapting to emerging threats and evolving operational requirements. The UAE has recognised the importance of investing in research and development (R&D) to stay at the forefront of defence technology.

Establishing institutions such as the Emirates Defence Industries Company (EDIC) and the Mohammed Bin Rashid Space Centre (MBRSC) illustrates the country's commitment to nurturing local expertise and capabilities. Developing advanced defence systems, including advanced uncrewed aerial vehicles (UAVs), missile defence systems, armoured vehicles, and naval vessels, has propelled the UAE's armed forces to new heights of technological sophistication.

National defence budgets also bear the weight of defence Emiratisation efforts. Defensive expenditure naturally increases as the UAE invests in R&D, infrastructure, and acquiring local defence technologies. However, this investment strengthens the nation's defence capabilities and creates a ripple effect on the national economy. Developing a robust defence industry stimulates local employment, encourages technology transfer, and nurtures a culture of innovation. The UAE has wisely focused on creating an ecosystem that supports the growth of the defence industry, including establishing specialised industrial zones such as the Tawazun Economic Council's Al Dhafra Defence Zone and the Dubai South Aerospace Supply Chain Complex. These zones provide a nurturing environment for defence companies to flourish, attracting foreign investment and fostering the development of local talent.

Furthermore, exports from successful defence Emiratisation projects can contribute to the UAE's overall economic growth and diversification. The UAE can enter the global defence market by establishing a reputation for producing high-quality defence equipment and technologies, generating revenues and expanding its influence. The country has already made strides in this direction, with defence companies like EDGE emerging as significant players in the global defence industry. The UAE's defence exports extend beyond arms and equipment, as the nation also exports knowledge and expertise in defence-related areas such as cybersecurity and satellite technology. This creates avenues for international collaboration and cooperation, further strengthening the UAE's regional and global defence partner position.

The geopolitical ramifications of defence Emiratisation in the UAE are equally significant. As the UAE develops its defence industry capabilities, it enhances its national security. It has become a regional hub for defence manufacturing and technology development. The country's strategic location and stable business environment make it an attractive destination for international defence companies looking to establish partnerships and access the growing Middle East defence market. The UAE's endeavours in defence Emiratisation are not limited to domestic efforts alone; the country actively seeks collaboration with international defence companies and research institutions to leverage global expertise, promote knowledge transfer, and enhance its defence capabilities.

This cementing of the UAE's position as a critical player in the Gulf region's security architecture strengthens its relationships and partnerships with regional actors. These collaborations extend beyond arms transfers and defence cooperation agreements, involving joint military exercises, training programmes, and intelligence sharing. The UAE's defence Emiratisation efforts have created a foundation for deeper partnerships, allowing the country to contribute effectively to regional security initiatives. Examples of this commitment can be seen in the UAE's participation in the Saudi-led coalition against Houthi rebels in Yemen and its role in international counterterrorism operations.

Therefore, defence Emiratisation in the UAE holds immense significance, with implications for national security, defence strategies, military capabilities, national defence budgets, the national economy, and the broader geopolitical context. The UAE's pursuit of a self-reliant defence industry aligns with the country's aspirations for economic diversification and technological innovation. Developing local defence capabilities and fostering local talent and expertise enhances the UAE's defence readiness, strengthens national security, and increases global influence.

The nation's commitment to defence Emiratisation is a blueprint for other regional actors looking to improve their defence industries and contribute to regional stability.

A. Background

The United Arab Emirates (UAE) has undergone a remarkable transformation in recent years, emerging as a critical player in the defence industry. Historically, the country heavily imported defence equipment and technologies from foreign suppliers to meet national security requirements. However, recognising the need for self-sufficiency and strategic autonomy, the UAE has embarked on a journey of defence Emiratisation.

The transformation of the UAE's defence industry has been driven by various factors, each with its significance. Firstly, there is a solid economic impetus to reduce dependency on imports and nurture a robust local defence sector that can contribute to the country's economic growth. The UAE, primarily fuelled by its vast oil reserves, has long been an economic powerhouse in the region. However, the country's leadership has recognised the importance of diversifying its economy to ensure sustainable growth. The UAE aims to stimulate local industries, create jobs, and attract foreign investments by developing domestic defence capabilities. This drive aligns with the broader national vision of diversifying the economy and reducing reliance on hydrocarbon resources.

Secondly, the UAE has ambitious technological aspirations. By cultivating a local defence industry, the country seeks to acquire advanced technologies, enhance its research and development capabilities, and develop a skilled workforce in defence and security. Simultaneously, this focus on technological development allows the UAE to become a knowledge-based economy, driving innovation and scientific progress in various domains. Building such technological capabilities will contribute to national defence and create spill-over effects for other sectors, fostering innovation, knowledge transfer, and technological advancements across the UAE's economy.

Thirdly, the UAE's efforts towards defence Emiratisation are motivated by geopolitical considerations. The Arabian Gulf region has experienced political instability and security challenges recently. In this context, the UAE aims to develop a self-reliant defence sector that swiftly responds to emerging threats and contributes to regional stability. The UAE seeks to bolster its strategic autonomy by reducing dependence on external suppliers and ensuring its defence needs are met even during global uncertainty. This pursuit of self-reliance is particularly crucial given the country's standing as a regional hub for trade and finance, making it vulnerable to potential security disruptions.

Furthermore, the UAE's drive for defence Emiratisation is not isolated from evolving regional security concerns. The rise of non-state actors, transnational terrorism, and proxy conflicts have reshaped the security dynamics of the Gulf region. As a responsible regional player, the UAE recognises the need to develop a strong defence capability to respond effectively to these challenges. By cultivating local defence capabilities, the UAE aims to position itself as a reliable partner in enhancing regional security cooperation and contributing to collective defence efforts.

The UAE's defence Emiratisation efforts encompass various vital components, including a focus on research and development, local production, technology transfer, and strategic partnerships with international defence firms. The country has invested significantly in establishing research and development centres to promote innovation and local technological advancements. Additionally, the UAE has forged partnerships and joint ventures with international defence industry leaders, facilitating knowledge transfer, skill development, and technology absorption.

The purpose of this book is to provide a comprehensive analysis of the UAE's defence Emiratisation efforts. It will delve into the motivations behind this transformation, its implications for national security and defence strategies, the performance of the national armed forces, the impact on national defence budgets, and the broader economic implications. Additionally, the book will explore the geopolitical ramifications of the UAE's defence Emiratisation for the Gulf region and its relations with international actors.

This book seeks to contribute to scholarly discussions on defence industry development, national security, and regional dynamics through a multidimensional examination of the UAE's defence Emiratisation journey. It aims to provide valuable insights for policymakers, defence experts, and researchers interested in understanding the transformation of the UAE's defence sector and its implications within a broader regional and global context. By shedding light on these complex aspects, the book portrays the UAE as an emerging force in the defence industry. It analyses its aspirations to take a prominent role in regional security affairs. By examining the economic, technological, and geopolitical factors driving the UAE's defence Emiratisation, this book aims to highlight the significance of the UAE's journey for regional security and defence autonomy and its potential implications for global defence industry dynamics.

B. Significance of Defense Emiratisation

In recent years, defence Emiratisation has gained significant importance for the United Arab Emirates (UAE) as it endeavours to reduce its dependence on foreign defence imports and develop its own domestic defence capabilities. This chapter delves deeper into the significance of defence Emiratisation in the UAE, comprehensively analysing why it has become a national priority.

One of the primary reasons for the UAE's focus on defence Emiratisation is the desire to bolster its national security. The region in which the UAE is situated has experienced significant geopolitical shifts and ongoing conflicts. As a result, the UAE recognises that it must have a robust defence capability to protect its borders, defend against potential threats, and ensure stability within the region. By building domestic defence capabilities, the UAE strengthens its ability to respond effectively to evolving regional dynamics, thus reinforcing its national security posture.

Economic diversification is another crucial factor driving defence Emiratisation in the UAE. Historically, the UAE has relied heavily on oil revenues, making it vulnerable to fluctuations in global oil prices. To reduce this vulnerability and achieve long-term sustainable growth, the country has been actively working to diversify its economy and stimulate other sectors. Developing a strong defence industry is seen as a means to achieve economic diversification, create jobs, foster innovation, and generate new revenue streams. By promoting local defence production, the UAE aims to boost its manufacturing sector, attract foreign investment, and contribute to the overall development of a knowledge-based economy.

Technological advancement is also a key driver of defence Emiratisation efforts in the UAE. The country has recognised the importance of acquiring and integrating advanced technologies into its defence sector to enhance its capabilities and stay ahead in an increasingly complex global security landscape. By investing in research and development (R&D), innovation, and the adoption of emerging technologies, the UAE aims to acquire cutting-edge defence solutions and establish itself as a technological powerhouse. This serves national security interests and contributes to the UAE's overall technological landscape, spurring advancements across multiple industries.

In pursuit of defence Emiratisation, the UAE has implemented a comprehensive strategy encompassing various initiatives. Establishing the Emirates Defence Industries Company (EDIC) as a conglomerate of defence companies is critical in consolidating the national defence sector. EDIC's mandate includes coordinating efforts, leveraging synergies, and fostering collaboration between entities involved in defence production. This initiative streamlines the UAE's defence industry, reduces duplication, and improves efficiency.

Furthermore, the UAE has actively sought partnerships and collaborations with international defence manufacturers to acquire knowledge and technical expertise. These partnerships have become joint ventures, licencing agreements, and technology transfer programmes. By collaborating with established defence industry players, the UAE has gained access to advanced defence technologies and manufacturing processes, rapidly advancing its domestic manufacturing capabilities. These collaborations contribute to developing local capabilities and lay the groundwork for the UAE to become a global hub for defence manufacturing, maintenance, and servicing.

Beyond producing weapons and military equipment, the UAE's defence Emiratisation efforts prioritise human capital development. Establishing specialised training and research institutes provides education and vocational training in defence-related fields. By cultivating a skilled workforce, the UAE ensures that it has the necessary expertise to support the growing defence industry, including research and development, system integration, and maintenance. These investments in human capital contribute to the UAE's overall knowledge economy, fostering innovation and creating a sustainable talent pool.

To sum up, the significance of defence Emiratisation for the UAE extends beyond mere economic or technological considerations. It is a multifaceted approach that enhances national security, promotes economic diversification, drives technological advancement, and addresses regional security concerns. The UAE's commitment to defence Emiratisation, evident through various initiatives, partnerships, and investments, underscores its determination to build a self-reliant and robust defence industry. The UAE strengthens its sovereignty, advances its strategic autonomy, and contributes to regional stability by reducing its dependency on foreign defence imports.

C. Purpose and Scope of the Book

Background

Defence Emiratisation refers to developing and producing defence technologies and capabilities within a country's borders rather than relying on imports. The United Arab Emirates (UAE), a country located in the Arabian Peninsula, has embarked on a significant journey towards achieving defence Emiratisation. This chapter introduces the topic and provides an in-depth overview of the book's scope and objectives.

OBJECTIVES

The primary objective of this book is to provide a comprehensive analysis of defence Emiratisation in the UAE and its significance in the country's overall defence strategy. By delving into various aspects and dimensions of this topic, readers will understand the motivations, implications, and impact of the UAE's drive for self-reliance in defence capabilities.

MOTIVATIONS FOR DEFENCE EMIRATISATION

The motivations behind the UAE's pursuit of defence Emiratisation are multifaceted and interconnected. Economic factors play a significant role as the country aims to develop a robust defence industry, contributing to its overall economic diversification and job creation goals. By nurturing a domestic defence industry, the UAE seeks to reduce its reliance on imports and retain more defence spending within its economy.

Technological ambitions also motivate the UAE's drive for Emiratisation. The country aims to enhance its technological capabilities, foster innovation, and become a regional leader in defence research and development by developing local technologies. This strengthens the UAE's defence posture and positions it as a hub for technological advancements in the region.

Geopolitical considerations underpin the UAE's pursuit of defence Emiratisation. The country aims to enhance its strategic autonomy and reduce vulnerabilities to external pressures. By developing its defence capabilities, the UAE seeks to diversify its defence supply chains, safeguard its national security, and reduce dependencies on foreign suppliers amidst a changing geopolitical landscape.

Moreover, defence Emiratisation is driven by the UAE's desire to strengthen its domestic industrial base. The country aims to create high-skilled jobs by developing a local defence industry and boosting its manufacturing capabilities. This contributes to long-term economic resilience and reduces the country's reliance on oil revenues, fostering economic diversification.

Regional security concerns further drive the UAE's pursuit of Emiratisation. The country faces various security challenges, including territorial disputes, terrorism threats, and regional instability. By developing local defence capabilities, the UAE aims to enhance its readiness and resilience to address these security challenges effectively within its borders and in collaboration with regional partners.

SCOPE OF THE BOOK

This book comprehensively analyses defence Emiratisation in the UAE, examining its motivations, implications, and impact from various perspectives. The following aspects will be explored:

National Security Implications: The book will analyse how defence Emiratisation contributes to the UAE's national security objectives. The country aims to enhance its strategic autonomy, strengthen its defence resilience, and adapt to evolving geopolitical shifts by reducing dependencies on foreign suppliers. It will delve into the developed defence capabilities, including advanced military systems, intelligence capabilities, and localised manufacturing capabilities.

Evolution of Military Doctrines: This book will examine how defence Emiratisation has influenced the evolution of the UAE's military doctrines. The country has effectively transformed its military strategies and approaches to address emerging threats by integrating local technologies and adapting to localised defence capabilities. It will explore the alignment between technology development and the army doctrine, emphasising innovation's role in shaping the UAE's future defence landscape.

Performance Evaluation of National Armed Forces: This book will evaluate the performance of the UAE's national armed forces after implementing defence Emiratisation measures. It will highlight the enhanced capabilities achieved through developing local defence technologies while addressing the challenges and opportunities encountered during this process. The book will examine how these enhanced capabilities have impacted the UAE's armed forces' overall readiness, effectiveness, and interoperability.

Financial Implications: The book will analyse the economic aspects of defence Emiratisation, including the allocation of resources, cost-benefit analysis, and the impact on the national defence budgets. It will explore the investments in research and development, infrastructure, and human capital and assess their long-term financial sustainability. The book will also examine the economic benefits of developing a domestic defence industry, such as job creation, technology transfer, and export potential.

Economic Impacts: This book will explore the broader implications of defence Emiratisation for the national economy. It will examine how this strategy contributes to UAE's economic diversification, job creation, and skill development. By assessing the financial impacts of defence Emiratisation, readers will gain insights into the interconnected nature of defence and the economy in the UAE. The book will also discuss the potential for the defence industry to become a driver of innovation and technological advancements in other sectors, fostering a knowledge-based economy.

Geopolitical Ramifications: This book will consider the geopolitical ramifications of defence Emiratisation for the Gulf region. It will analyse how the UAE's pursuit of self-reliance recalibrates alliances, influences power dynamics within the Gulf, and impacts regional and international relations. The book will examine the potential for defence Emiratisation to enhance the UAE's role as a regional security provider and contribute to stability in the Gulf region.

This book will provide a comprehensive and multidimensional analysis of defence Emiratisation in the UAE by encompassing these aspects. It aims to contribute to the existing literature on defence studies, economic development, and regional security. It offers valuable insights to scholars and researchers, policymakers, defence industry professionals, and anyone interested in defence affairs in the UAE and beyond.

II

Historical Context

The historical context of defence Emiratisation in the UAE is crucial in understanding the country's journey towards reducing dependence on foreign defence imports. For a significant period, the UAE relied heavily on foreign suppliers to fulfil its military needs. This reliance can be traced back to the early days of the UAE's formation when it lacked the necessary infrastructure, technological capabilities, and skilled workforce to develop and produce its defence equipment.

At its inception in 1971, the UAE faced challenges in establishing a robust defence sector due to its limited population and resources. This compelled the Emirati leadership to seek alliances and partnerships with established military powers. The initial years saw a reliance on countries like the United Kingdom and France for defence equipment, including fighter jets, tanks, naval vessels, and air defence systems.

The UAE's vision of developing a solid defence capability was significantly boosted in 1975 when it signed a defence agreement with the United States, which marked the beginning of a long-standing partnership.

This agreement paved the way for the UAE Armed Forces to acquire advanced military hardware, such as the F-16 fighters, Apache attack helicopters, and missile defence systems, contributing to the UAE's military modernisation efforts.

Throughout the 1980s and 1990s, the UAE's defence budget experienced substantial growth, fuelled by its rapid economic development and increasing regional security concerns. The government recognised the need to address emerging threats and challenges while diversifying the UAE's economy beyond oil and gas. This period witnessed an intensive focus on military modernisation programmes, which enabled the UAE to acquire state-of-the-art defence technologies and capabilities from its foreign partners.

The UAE took notable steps towards technology transfer and knowledge acquisition in line with its ambition to enhance local defence capabilities. Joint ventures and collaborations with leading international defence companies were established, allowing the UAE to benefit from the expertise and experience of its foreign partners. Notable projects included the development of the UAE's first military avionics company, Galair, in partnership with French defence firms, and the Gulf Aircraft Maintenance Company (GAMCO), which collaborated with Lockheed Martin, Boeing, and British Aerospace to support the maintenance and upgrade of aircraft fleets.

The UAE's efforts to reduce dependence on foreign defence imports gained momentum in 1999 with establishing the Tawazun Economic Council. Tawazun served as a catalyst for developing local defence industries, focusing on technology transfer, investment in research and development, and fostering strategic partnerships between local and international defence companies. Initiatives such as the Emirates Advanced Research and Technology Holding (EARTH) and Emirates Defence Industries Company (EDIC) were launched to enhance local

R&D capabilities and facilitate government, academia, and industry collaboration.

The UAE also made significant investments in human capital development to support the growth of its defence industry. It established specialised educational institutions, such as the Khalifa University of Science and Technology and the National Defence College, offering engineering and technology-focused programmes. These institutions provided a steady stream of well-trained graduates with the skills needed to contribute effectively to the local defence manufacturing sector.

The UAE's defence Emiratisation efforts have expanded into emerging and high-tech sectors in the recent decade. The country has invested in cybersecurity, unmanned systems, space technology, and artificial intelligence, recognising their increasing significance in modern warfare. Strategic partnerships and joint ventures with global leaders in these fields have facilitated knowledge transfer and helped develop local capabilities.

To further boost the Emiratisation of defence, the UAE launched the "Made in the UAE" campaign in 2014. This initiative aimed to promote local defence manufacturing, reduce import reliance, and nurture homegrown defence companies. Establishing defence industrial parks and free zones, such as the Abu Dhabi Ship Building (ADSB), Dubai South Aerospace, and NIMR Automotive, provided dedicated spaces for research, development, and manufacturing, fostering innovation and collaboration.

In conclusion, the historical context of the UAE's defence industry reveals a phased transition from heavy reliance on foreign defence imports to a strategic pursuit of self-sufficiency. The UAE's commitment to economic diversification, technological advancement, and regional security has driven the development of its local defence capabilities.

The UAE aims to strengthen its national security, foster innovation, and propel its defence industry onto the global stage through targeted investments, technology transfer, and strategic partnerships.

A. Evolution of the UAE's Defence Industry

The United Arab Emirates (UAE) has a rich history when it comes to the development of its defence industry. This chapter will delve into the evolution of the UAE's defence industry, tracing its origins and subsequent growth over the years.

The early stages of the UAE's defence industry can be attributed to the country's formation in 1971. At that time, the UAE relied heavily on imports to meet its defence needs. The government established partnerships with various countries, such as the United Kingdom, France, and the United States, to supply it with the necessary military equipment.

However, this heavy reliance on foreign suppliers was seen as a vulnerability for the UAE. It became apparent that to have a reliable and sustainable defence industry, the UAE would need to develop its indigenised capabilities.

The turning point in the evolution of the UAE's defence industry came with establishing the UAE Armed Forces in 1976. The armed forces played a critical role in driving the development of the defence industry, as it recognised the importance of self-sufficiency in defence production.

To kickstart this process, the UAE invested in research and development (R&D) initiatives related to defence technologies. This involved collaborating with international defence companies to acquire knowledge and expertise in aerospace, naval, and land-based defence systems.

One notable partnership that contributed significantly to the UAE's defence industry's growth was the collaboration with France. In the 1990s, the UAE signed a strategic cooperation agreement with France, which paved the way for transferring advanced defence technologies and capabilities. This partnership led to the establishment of joint ventures, such as the Emirates Advanced Investments Group (EAIG), which focused on R&D in advanced technologies and defence systems.

The establishment of local defence companies and industries marked the next phase in the evolution of the UAE's defence industry. One of the most notable examples is the Emirates Defence Industries Company (EDIC), launched in 2014. EDIC brought together various defence entities and helped streamline the defence industry in the UAE.

Under EDIC's umbrella, several key defence companies were formed, including the Abu Dhabi Ship Building Company (ADSB), which specialises in constructing and repairing naval vessels, and the Tawazun Economic Council, which focuses on developing defence industrial capabilities.

In addition to these efforts, the UAE also focused on enhancing its domestic defence manufacturing capabilities. Through technology transfers and joint ventures with international defence companies, the UAE was able to develop its local defence products, ranging from armoured vehicles to drones and even naval vessels.

For instance, the UAE partnered with international defence companies, such as Boeing and Lockheed Martin, to establish joint ventures like the Advanced Military Maintenance Repair and Overhaul Centre (AMMROC) and STRATA Manufacturing. These partnerships have enabled the UAE to enhance its capabilities in aircraft maintenance, repair, manufacturing, and production of advanced aircraft components.

Over the years, the UAE's defence industry has become more self-reliant and capable of meeting the country's defence needs. It has achieved several significant milestones, including the production of the region's first local military helicopter, the Nimr multipurpose armoured vehicle, and the development of advanced drone technologies for surveillance and military applications.

The UAE's defence industry has expanded its reach beyond domestic requirements, becoming an exporter of defence products and services. This expansion has been facilitated by the strategic acquisition of foreign companies and the establishment of joint ventures abroad.

The acquisition of companies like AM General, the manufacturer of the iconic Humvee, has allowed the UAE to tap into international markets and diversify its defence portfolio.

Furthermore, the UAE has sought to develop its defence manufacturing base through initiatives like the Defence Manufacturing Management Programme (DMMAP). This programme has provided local defence companies with the necessary tools and expertise to enhance their manufacturing capabilities and increase their competitiveness in the global market.

The evolution of the UAE's defence industry has given the country greater autonomy and control over its defence capabilities and has had broader implications for its national security and regional standing.

It has positioned the UAE as a key player in the defence sector and has enhanced its military capabilities, ensuring its ability to protect its national interests.

In recent years, the UAE has strongly emphasised innovation and cutting-edge technologies in its defence industry. It has established innovation hubs like the Khalifa University Robotics Institute to foster research and development in autonomous systems, artificial intelligence, and robotics in the defence sector. This focus on innovation has allowed the UAE to stay at the forefront of technological advancements in defence and keep up with the evolving nature of warfare.

Moreover, the UAE has also prioritised cybersecurity as a crucial component of national defence.

The country has invested in developing cybersecurity capabilities to protect its critical infrastructures, government entities, and defence systems from emerging cyber threats. It has established entities like the UAE Cyber Security Council and Cybersecurity Centre of Excellence to enhance its cybersecurity defences and collaborate with international partners.

The UAE's defence industry has also played a significant role in fostering economic diversification and job creation.

With the establishment of local defence companies and developing defence manufacturing capabilities, the industry has created numerous high-skilled job opportunities for Emirati citizens. This has contributed to the country's economic growth and helped build a knowledge-based economy as Emiratis gain expertise in advanced defence technologies and systems.

In conclusion, the evolution of the UAE's defence industry has been a dynamic and far-reaching process driven by the country's desire to become self-sufficient in meeting its defence needs.

Through strategic investments in research and development, the establishment of local defence companies, the development of local defence manufacturing capabilities, and strategic partnerships and acquisitions, the UAE has transformed itself into a strong and independent player in the global defence industry. Its focus on innovation and cybersecurity further solidifies its position as a forward-thinking and technologically advanced defence industry.

B. Previous Dependence on Foreign Defence Imports

In the early years of its existence, the United Arab Emirates (UAE) experienced a heavy reliance on foreign defence imports to meet its military needs. This dependence stemmed from the country's nascent defence industry, limited local capabilities, and the imperative to rapidly build capable armed forces. However, it brought about significant economic, strategic, and geopolitical implications, prompting the UAE to embark on a transformative journey of defence Emiratisation.

Economically, the UAE's reliance on foreign defence imports resulted in substantial capital outflows. Enormous sums were spent purchasing advanced weapons systems, equipment, and technologies from international suppliers. These expenditures strained the national budget, limiting resource allocation for critical developmental areas such as infrastructure, healthcare, and education. Recognising this, the UAE aimed to reduce its import dependency, enabling financial resources to be redirected towards its own defence industry and simultaneously addressing domestic socio-economic needs.

Moreover, the dependence on foreign defence imports hindered the UAE's strategic autonomy. Any disruption in supply chains, adverse political developments, or embargoes imposed by supplier nations could have potentially endangered the country's defence readiness. This vulnerability led the Emirati leadership to prioritise the development of a self-sufficient defence industry capable of meeting the country's evolving security needs without external limitations.

Furthermore, the dependency on foreign defence imports created a technological gap between the UAE's armed forces and its regional competitors. Relying on external suppliers limited access to the latest advancements in defence technologies, hindering the country's ability to keep pace with emerging threats. It also restricted opportunities for technological innovation and knowledge transfer within the nation. Recognising the importance of technological self-sufficiency, the UAE sought to build its local research and development capabilities, nurturing a culture of innovation and fostering collaborations with global partners to bridge the technological gap.

In addition to the economic and strategic factors, the UAE's dependence on foreign defence imports had notable geopolitical implications. The acquisition of defence systems from other countries tied the UAE's defence capabilities to the interests and policies of the supplying nations. This made the country vulnerable to political pressures and potential interference in its defence affairs. To safeguard its sovereignty and enhance its geopolitical manoeuvrability, the UAE recognised the need to develop local defence capabilities, reducing reliance on external suppliers and becoming a more self-reliant actor on the global stage.

The UAE initiated a comprehensive defence Emiratisation programme to respond to these challenges. This multifaceted approach aimed to develop local defence capabilities, foster research and development in the defence sector, and nurture a local defence industry.

It entailed creating a conducive ecosystem for developing defence-related innovation, manufacturing, and technological advancements within the country.

The transformation of the UAE's defence industry was motivated by numerous factors. Ensuring national security and reducing dependence on external suppliers were primary drivers. The UAE sought to provide a consistent supply of defence equipment, technologies, and spare parts by fostering local capabilities. This would enable the country to maintain a high level of defence readiness, enhance its response capabilities, and safeguard against potential disruptions caused by geopolitical dynamics or supply chain vulnerabilities.

Moreover, developing a local defence industry allowed the UAE to diversify its economy. The country envisioned building a vibrant defence sector capable of generating employment opportunities, attracting foreign investment, and nurturing technological innovation. This diversification strategy aligned with the UAE's vision of transitioning from an oil-dependent economy to a knowledge-based and innovation-driven society. The defence industry offered ample potential for job creation, skills development, and the fostering of a competitive and sustainable economy.

Furthermore, defence Emiratisation allowed the UAE to forge strategic partnerships and cooperation agreements with other nations. The UAE became an attractive partner for technology transfers, joint research and development projects, and collaborative defence initiatives by developing its defence capabilities. Through these partnerships, the UAE not only enhanced its defence capabilities but also positioned itself as a reliable and capable defence collaborator in the international arena. By sharing resources, knowledge, and expertise with global counterparts, the UAE aimed to create mutually beneficial relationships that would accelerate the growth of its defence industry.

In conclusion, the UAE's previous dependence on foreign defence imports had wide-ranging economic, strategic, and geopolitical implications. Acknowledging the challenges posed by this reliance, the UAE embarked on a transformative journey of defence Emiratisation to reduce its dependency on external suppliers and foster the growth of a robust and self-sufficient defence industry. This holistic approach aimed to enhance national security, diversify the economy, and establish the UAE as a critical player in the global defence arena.

C. Catalysts for Change

The process of defence Emiratisation in the UAE has not occurred in isolation. Several catalysts have played a significant role in shaping the nation's determination to develop its defence industry. This chapter explores the key factors that have driven and facilitated this change.

One important catalyst has been the UAE's growing economic strength. Over the past few decades, the UAE has experienced remarkable economic growth and diversification, driven by its strategic vision and forward-thinking policies. Its development into a global trade, finance, and tourism hub has placed it at the forefront of the region's emerging economies. This economic prosperity has provided the nation with the financial resources necessary to invest in defence capabilities and develop its defence industry.

Recognising that a vigorous defence sector contributes to national security and overall stability, the UAE leadership has made significant investments in research and development, infrastructure, and human capital, laying the foundation for a robust local defence sector. Establishing specialised defence zones, such as the Tawazun Industrial Park, has created an enabling environment for defence companies by providing state-of-the-art facilities, tax incentives, and access to diverse support services.

Technological aspirations have also been a significant catalyst for change in the UAE's defence sector. The nation has long been driven by its leadership's ambition for innovation and development, which is evident in the diverse projects and initiatives launched in various sectors. In the defence realm, the UAE has sought to acquire cutting-edge defence technologies to enhance its military capabilities. However, continued dependence on foreign suppliers limited the UAE's ability to access and control advanced technologies fully.

This realisation became instrumental in fuelling the push for Emiratisation, as it aimed to reduce reliance on foreign sources and acquire the necessary knowledge and expertise to develop its defence technologies. The UAE has strategically partnered with renowned global manufacturers and defence contractors to achieve these technological aspirations. These collaborations have facilitated technology transfer, joint ventures, and knowledge exchange, allowing the UAE to develop its local expertise and capabilities.

The government's commitment to research and development has also fostered the growth of local defence technology companies, which have made significant strides in developing advanced systems and solutions tailored to the nation's specific requirements. For instance, the Emirates Defence Industries Company (EDIC), established in 2014, is a strategic platform for consolidating and coordinating the UAE's defence industries. Through its diverse subsidiaries and collaborations, EDIC is driving innovation, enhancing local manufacturing capabilities, and supporting the development of a highly skilled workforce.

Another catalyst for change is the shifting geopolitical landscape of the region. Like many countries in the Gulf, the UAE has faced significant security challenges, including regional conflicts and threats posed by non-state actors.

These challenges have underscored the need for self-reliance and the capacity to respond to emerging security threats swiftly.

By developing its defence capabilities, the UAE seeks to become more self-sufficient in addressing security concerns, thus safeguarding its interests and enhancing its regional influence. The UAE has consistently reinforced its commitment to security by maintaining a comprehensive and technologically advanced military. This commitment is evident in significant defence procurements, including acquiring advanced fighter jets, missile defence systems, naval vessels, and unmanned aerial vehicles.

Furthermore, the UAE's drive for defence Emiratisation is also motivated by its goal of reinforcing regional security cooperation. The nation aims to establish itself as a leader in defence innovation and contribute to collective regional security efforts. By developing local defence industries, the UAE can strengthen military ties with its regional partners, promote interoperability, and foster collaboration necessary for countering common threats.

This approach aligns with the UAE's broader foreign policy objectives, emphasising building strong partnerships to achieve regional stability and security. The nation actively participates in joint military exercises, training programmes, and information-sharing initiatives with its Gulf Cooperation Council (GCC) counterparts and international allies such as the United States, France, and the United Kingdom.

The commitment to defence Emiratisation extends beyond achieving self-sufficiency. The UAE also recognises the economic benefits of a thriving defence industry. By nurturing local capacities and expertise, the UAE can create high-skilled jobs, attract foreign direct investment, and foster a knowledge-based economy.

The defence industry can also serve as a catalyst for innovation and technological advancement in other sectors, leading to a multiplier effect on the UAE's overall economic growth.

For example, the defence sector's technological advancements have contributed to advances in other industries, including aerospace, cybersecurity, and advanced manufacturing. The UAE's investment in defence research and development has established innovation hubs and centres of excellence, such as the Mohamed bin Zayed University of Artificial Intelligence and the Mohammed bin Rashid Space Centre. These institutions support defence-related research and promote collaboration with academia, industry, and international partners, fostering technological innovation and knowledge transfer that benefits the broader economy.

The UAE's defence Emiratisation efforts have also been bolstered by the nation's robust educational and vocational training institutions. The government has invested heavily in developing local talent and promoting STEM education to ensure a skilled workforce capable of driving technological advancements in the defence sector. A strong emphasis has been placed on developing homegrown talent in engineering, computer science, and applied sciences.

Additionally, initiatives such as scholarships, grants, and collaborative programmes with leading international academic institutions have facilitated the transfer of knowledge and expertise, further enhancing the UAE's defence capabilities. The UAE's commitment to human capital development is evident in establishments like the Khalifa University, which offers specialised defence-related education and research opportunities, and the National Defence College, which provides advanced strategic-level education to military and civilian leaders.

Ultimately, combining these catalysts has propelled the UAE towards defence Emiratisation.

The nation's economic strength, technological ambitions, the evolving regional security landscape, and the desire for greater regional collaboration have all contributed to the decision to develop a strong defence industry.

Embracing these catalysts for change, the UAE is poised to transform itself from a consumer of defence technology to a producer and exporter, establishing itself as a renowned player in the global defence market. Through strategic investments, partnerships, and a focus on innovation and talent development, the UAE is set to safeguard its national interests securely, contribute to regional security, and drive economic growth in the defence sector and beyond.

III

The Motivations Behind Defence Emiratisation

Defence Emiratisation, the process of developing and producing military equipment domestically, is driven by various motivations in the United Arab Emirates (UAE). These motivations can be grouped into economic factors, technological ambitions, geopolitical considerations, and regional security concerns, all contributing to the country's vision for a self-sufficient and technologically advanced defence industry.

A. ECONOMIC FACTORS:

Economically, defence Emiratisation offers significant advantages to the UAE. By reducing reliance on foreign defence imports, the country can have greater control over its defence budget and reduce the outflow of funds to other nations. Allocating resources towards the development of the defence industry creates a positive economic ripple effect with the creation of jobs, growth of local businesses, and the attraction of foreign direct investment. Embracing defence Emiratisation strengthens the UAE's economy. It builds resilience by diversifying its industrial base, reducing vulnerabilities to external economic shocks, and promoting self-sustaining growth.

B. TECHNOLOGICAL AMBITIONS:

Defence Emiratisation aligns with the UAE's broader vision of becoming a global leader in technology and innovation. The country can acquire cutting-edge technologies and expertise in critical defence areas by investing in research and development within the defence sector. This includes advancements in aerospace, shipbuilding, cyber defence, artificial intelligence, and advanced weapon systems. The result of homegrown defence technologies enhances the UAE's overall defence capabilities and stimulates the growth of associated civilian industries. These advancements contribute to developing the UAE's industrial and knowledge-based sectors, driving sustainable economic growth and reinforcing its position as a technological powerhouse.

C. GEOPOLITICAL CONSIDERATIONS:

From a geopolitical standpoint, defence Emiratisation provides the UAE with greater strategic autonomy and fosters a sense of national pride. By developing its defence capabilities, the country reduces the vulnerabilities of relying solely on foreign defence suppliers. This ensures the UAE can maintain its defence readiness even during international conflicts or political tensions. Independence in defence procurement enables the UAE to shape its defence policies, aligning them with its national interests and long-term strategic goals. It also allows the country to pursue its foreign policy objectives without overly dependent on external actors. By diversifying its defence suppliers and fostering strategic partnerships, the UAE strengthens its diplomatic position. It reinforces its status as a regional power.

D. REGIONAL SECURITY CONCERNS:

Defence Emiratisation plays a vital role in enhancing regional security and stability. The UAE's investment in its defence industry enables it to contribute to the collective security of the Gulf region. The UAE can actively participate in joint defence operations, share expertise with neighbouring countries, and foster regional military cooperation by developing advanced defence capabilities. The country plays a critical role in deterring potential adversaries and ensuring the security of vital sea lanes and maritime territories. Defence collaboration with regional allies strengthens collective security efforts, facilitates interoperability, and enhances regional defence capabilities, ultimately contributing to the stability and peace of the Gulf region.

Furthermore, defence Emiratisation allows the UAE to project its diplomatic influence beyond regional boundaries. The UAE has become an attractive partner for defence collaboration and intergovernmental cooperation by showcasing its capabilities and technological advancements. This increases the UAE's visibility on the global stage and elevates its status as a reliable and capable security partner, contributing to its broader foreign policy objectives.

In conclusion, the motivations behind defence Emiratisation in the UAE are multi-faceted and interconnected, spanning economic growth, technological advancement, strategic autonomy, and regional security priorities. By reducing dependencies, enhancing defence capabilities, fostering innovation, and contributing to regional stability, the UAE aims to forge its path as a modern and self-reliant defence force. These motivations underscore the significance of defence Emiratisation as a fundamental component of the UAE's national defence strategy and broader regional and international engagement.

A. Economic Factors

The economic considerations surrounding defence Emiratisation efforts in the United Arab Emirates (UAE) are multifaceted and play a significant role in driving the country's pursuit of self-sufficiency in defence capabilities. This chapter delves deeper into the various economic factors contributing to the UAE's endeavours in defence Emiratisation.

Firstly, one of the primary motivations for defence Emiratisation is to boost the domestic economy. By establishing a robust defence industry, the UAE aims to create opportunities for job creation and skill development within the country. The defence sector is known for its high-tech and high-skilled nature, requiring specialised expertise. By developing a skilled workforce through defence Emiratisation, the UAE can reduce its reliance on foreign workers, enhance its industrial base, and stimulate economic growth. The demand for skilled labour in the defence industry can also lead to the formation of specialised training centres and institutes, further uplifting the human capital development in the country.

Moreover, defence Emiratisation catalyses economic diversification. The UAE has recognised the need to reduce its reliance on oil revenues and diversify the economy. By investing in defence industries and fostering technological innovation, the UAE aims to diversify its economic sectors. This diversification enhances financial stability and allows for developing a knowledge-based and innovation-driven economy.

The knowledge and expertise gained in defence Emiratisation can be applied to other sectors such as renewable energy, transportation, healthcare, and advanced manufacturing, fostering growth and reducing dependence on oil. The defence industry is a crucial engine for economic diversification and a stepping stone for the UAE's transition to a post-oil era.

Additionally, defence Emiratisation stimulates research and development (R&D) within the UAE. The defence sector thrives on continuous technological advancements to maintain a competitive edge. By investing in R&D, the UAE fosters an environment of innovation and technological advancement. This benefits the defence sector and has a spillover effect, improving technological capabilities in other areas. For instance, advances in defence-related technologies can be utilised in civilian applications such as aerospace, telecommunications, cybersecurity, and healthcare. The R&D investments can also attract global collaborations and partnerships, further enhancing the UAE's position as a hub for innovation, research, and development.

Furthermore, defence Emiratisation can positively impact the UAE's trade balance. Historically, the country has heavily relied on importing defence equipment and services, resulting in significant capital outflows. By transitioning towards self-sufficiency, the UAE can reduce its import dependency, thus retaining more defence expenditures within the domestic market. This can have a cascading effect on the national economy. Local businesses will benefit from government contracts and increased demand, leading to job creation, revenue, and economic growth. Moreover, the UAE can export its local defence products, generating additional revenue and strengthening its trade surplus. A strong defence industry will reduce the import-export imbalance, improving the country's overall economic position.

Moreover, establishing a robust defence industrial base contributes to the UAE's economic resilience.

As the country acquires local capabilities, it builds a competitive defence industry that meets domestic needs. This resilience is crucial for the UAE's national security, as it reduces vulnerability to supply chain disruptions, geopolitical tensions, and fluctuations in international markets. A strong defence industrial base also opens up opportunities for global collaboration and defence exports. The UAE can position itself as a reliable defence exporter, generating foreign exchange earnings and contributing to economic growth. This also enhances the country's strategic partnerships on a global scale, bringing in foreign direct investment and promoting technology transfer. International collaborations help the UAE gain access to advanced technologies and knowledge, enriching their defence capabilities further.

In conclusion, economic factors are crucial and multifaceted in driving the UAE's pursuit of defence Emiratisation. By boosting the domestic economy, diversifying economic sectors, stimulating R&D, improving the trade balance, and developing a robust defence industrial base, the UAE aims to achieve long-term financial sustainability and reduce its dependence on external sources for defence-related needs. These efforts contribute to the country's overall economic development, fostering innovation and job creation and positioning the UAE as a global player in the defence industry and technology. The economic benefits garnered through defence Emiratisation catalyse broader economic transformation and stability, reinforcing the UAE's position as an influential player in the region and the world.

B. Technological Ambitions

In the pursuit of defence Emiratisation, the United Arab Emirates (UAE) has set ambitious technological goals that go beyond traditional military capabilities. The aim is not only to reduce dependence on foreign defence technology but also to foster the development of a robust local defence industry that drives innovation, enhances national security, and stimulates economic growth. This chapter explores the UAE's technological ambitions in greater depth, delving into various dimensions of its strategic planning, investments, and prospects.

Recognising the importance of staying ahead in an increasingly digitised and interconnected world, the UAE has embarked on an extensive research and development (R&D) effort to acquire, innovate, and adapt cutting-edge defence technologies. The nation significantly emphasises emerging technologies such as artificial intelligence (AI), autonomous systems, and space technologies. The UAE's AI strategy focuses on developing AI-powered defence systems to enhance situational awareness, improve decision-making processes, and provide advanced analytics for mission planning and execution.

The UAE government has established specialised R&D centres, research institutes, and innovation hubs to support these efforts. One notable example is the Mohammed Bin Rashid Space Centre (MBRSC), dedicated to space research and exploration. MBRSC has made significant advancements in satellite technology, satellite imagery, and remote sensing, enabling the UAE to enhance its intelligence, surveillance, and reconnaissance capabilities. It has also facilitated the development of satellite-based communication systems, which ensure secure and reliable communication channels for defence operations.

In its pursuit of self-sufficiency, the UAE has strategically partnered with leading international defence companies to transfer technology and knowledge. Collaborations with companies like Lockheed Martin and BAE Systems have enabled the UAE to enhance its domestic defence capabilities and contribute to the global defence supply chain. These partnerships have resulted in technology-sharing agreements and joint ventures, allowing the UAE to benefit from advanced systems like advanced radar systems, electronic warfare capabilities, and state-of-the-art weapon systems.

Additionally, the UAE has proactively attracted leading global defence companies to establish their research and development hubs. This vision has materialised through technology parks such as the Abu Dhabi Technology Development Committee. These parks provide an ecosystem that fosters innovation and collaboration among academia, industry, and government entities, further propelling the country's technological advancements.

Furthermore, the UAE's technological ambitions extend beyond defence applications. The nation recognises the potential for economic diversification by leveraging advanced technologies across various sectors. For instance, the UAE's investments in AI and autonomous systems have allowed it to explore applications beyond defence, such as smart cities, transportation systems, and healthcare. This multi-dimensional approach ensures that technological advancements benefit national security and the broader economy.

To support these ambitions, the UAE has prioritised nurturing local talent in science, technology, engineering, and mathematics (STEM) fields through specialised education and training programmes. The nation understands that a skilled workforce drives technological advancements and innovation. Initiatives like the UAE Artificial Intelligence Camp allow exceptional students to explore advanced technologies, gain hands-on experience, and contribute to cutting-edge research in AI.

Looking ahead, the UAE's technological ambitions have the potential to position it as a global hub for defence technology innovation. By fostering a culture of innovation and entrepreneurship, the UAE aims to attract top talent, promote startups, and further diversify its economy. The country is focused on advancing its technological leadership by exploring disruptive technologies like quantum computing, advanced robotics, and next-generation connectivity.

In conclusion, the UAE's technological ambitions form a vital component of its broader goals to enhance national security, drive innovation, and stimulate economic growth. Through extensive investments in R&D, partnerships with global defence companies, and nurturing local talent, the UAE has laid a solid foundation for developing a local defence industry. By embracing emerging technologies, the UAE is poised to become a leading global player in defence technology innovation, contributing to the advancement of the sector while securing its defence capabilities and positioning itself as a technologically advanced nation.

C. Geopolitical Considerations

Economic factors or technological ambitions do not solely drive the defence Emiratisation process in the UAE. It is also heavily influenced by geopolitical considerations that shape the country's national security landscape. In a region characterised by political volatility and security challenges, the UAE has recognised the need for greater self-reliance in defence capabilities to navigate the complex geopolitical environment.

One of the primary geopolitical considerations driving defence Emiratisation in the UAE is the region's changing dynamics. The Middle East has long been a hotbed of geopolitical tensions and rivalries, and the UAE finds itself at the intersection of various regional conflicts and power struggles. These dynamics have intensified in recent years with the rise of non-state actors, sectarian divisions, and proxy conflicts. As a result, the UAE has witnessed a shifting balance of power and increasing uncertainties.

Traditional alliances and security arrangements the UAE has relied upon in the past have become more complex. The country has recognised that external military interventions may not always align with its national interests or security objectives. Moreover, defence imports from foreign suppliers can create vulnerabilities during regional instability.

In this context, defence Emiratisation ensures the UAE can maintain consistent defence preparedness regardless of external circumstances.

The UAE aims to ensure its strategic autonomy and reduce dependencies on external actors by developing its defence industry. This approach gives the country greater control over its defence procurement decisions, decreasing reliance on any single country or supplier. Geopolitical factors, such as changing alliances and international tensions, can impact the availability and reliability of defence imports. Therefore, building local defence capabilities allows the UAE more flexibility in responding to evolving geopolitical dynamics.

Another important consideration is the UAE's desire to establish itself as a regional power and contribute to collective security efforts. The country has actively participated in regional military coalitions and peacekeeping missions, such as the Saudi-led coalition in Yemen and UN peacekeeping missions. The UAE can meet its national security needs and contribute to regional stability by developing its defence industry.

The UAE seeks to provide technologically advanced defence equipment and services to neighbouring countries, enhancing their collective defence capabilities. This approach contributes to a sense of shared security and cooperation among Gulf Cooperation Council (GCC) states, enabling the UAE to shape regional security dynamics effectively and counter shared threats. By leading in defence Emiratisation efforts, the UAE aims to inspire other countries to develop their defence industries, thereby creating a network of self-reliant nations capable of collectively addressing regional security challenges.

Besides defence Emiratisation serves as a means for the UAE to project its influence on the international stage. By becoming a self-sufficient player in defence manufacturing and technology development, the UAE can expand its diplomatic reach and gain a stronger voice in global security discussions.

Advanced defence capabilities can lead to partnerships and collaborations with other countries, enabling the UAE to participate in joint research and development initiatives and contribute to global security norms and standards. This positioning allows the government to assert itself as a reliable and capable partner in international security cooperation, strengthening its geopolitical standing.

Moreover, defence Emiratisation offers economic diversification opportunities in line with the UAE's long-term goals. While the country has historically relied on oil revenue, the leadership recognises the need to transition towards a knowledge-based economy. Developing a robust defence industry promotes technology transfer and innovation, creates job opportunities, and enhances human capital development. The UAE aims to attract foreign investment and build a competitive defence industrial base that can pivot towards civilian technology sectors, contributing to overall economic growth and resilience.

However, defence Emiratisation has challenges and geopolitical risks. Developing advanced defence capabilities requires significant investment, technological expertise, and long-term commitment. The UAE must carefully navigate regional rivalries and geopolitical power struggles to avoid further antagonising other actors or escalating conflicts. Striking a balance between national defence priorities and regional dynamics is crucial to ensure that defence Emiratisation serves the UAE's national security interests and the broader stability of the Gulf region.

Furthermore, the UAE must manage technology transfer partnerships effectively. Balancing acquiring advanced defence technologies from foreign partners and developing domestic capabilities is essential. The UAE prioritises collaboration and joint ventures that allow for knowledge transfer and the development of local expertise. Building local defence capabilities also requires nurturing a skilled workforce and fostering a culture of innovation and resilience.

In conclusion, geopolitical considerations are crucial in the UAE's defence Emiratisation efforts. By reducing dependencies on foreign suppliers, asserting strategic autonomy, and contributing to regional security, the UAE aims to position itself as a critical player in the increasingly complex and volatile Gulf region. Understanding and managing the geopolitical implications of defence Emiratisation is essential for the UAE's long-term national security and regional stability. The country's pursuit of self-reliance in defence capabilities enhances its security. It enables it to shape the dynamics of regional security cooperation and exert influence on the global stage. Additionally, defence Emiratisation provides avenues for economic diversification, job creation, and technological development, aligning with the UAE's broader goals of transitioning towards a knowledge-based economy.

D. Regional Security Concerns

Regional security concerns play a crucial role in the defence Emiratisation efforts of the United Arab Emirates (UAE). Situated in a volatile and complex regional environment, the UAE faces many challenges that have significantly shaped its defence strategy and driven the development of local defence capabilities. Understanding these regional security concerns can give us deeper insights into the UAE's approach to safeguarding national security and contributing to regional stability.

One of the primary regional security concerns that have profoundly influenced the UAE's defence Emiratisation efforts is the threat posed by Iran. The historical tensions between the two countries, compounded by territorial disputes in the Abu Musa and Greater and Lesser Tunb islands, have heightened the UAE's focus on maritime security.

With its extensive coastline along the Persian Gulf and the strategic Strait of Hormuz—through which a significant portion of global oil trade passes—the UAE recognises the crucial importance of safeguarding its territorial waters, vital sea lanes, and economic interests.

The UAE has substantially invested in developing a robust naval and maritime defence infrastructure to address this persistent concern.

Efforts have been made to enhance the capabilities of the UAE Navy, Coast Guard, and Air Force through modernisation and the acquisition of advanced naval platforms, surface vessels, submarines, patrol boats, maritime surveillance systems, and complementing aerial assets. The country has also established advanced surveillance networks, such as command and control centres, radars, and monitoring stations, to detect and respond to potential threats. The UAE has also prioritised the development of its naval personnel by providing them with advanced training and technology to ensure proficiency in maritime operations.

The regional security concerns of the UAE are not limited to the immediate vicinity of its borders but also extend to neighbouring conflict zones. One such example is the war in Yemen, which poses a significant threat to the UAE's security due to its proximity and potential spill-over effects. The UAE has demonstrated its commitment to regional stability by actively participating in the Saudi-led coalition and supporting efforts to counter Houthi rebels in Yemen. Additionally, the UAE has worked towards building local defence capabilities to contribute effectively to these operations, including deploying specialised forces, intelligence sharing mechanisms, tactical training, and providing military aid to local forces. By doing so, the UAE aims to prevent the conflict from spilling into its territory and stabilise the wider region.

The UAE recognises the importance of enhancing its counter-terrorism capabilities to combat transnational threats. The presence of terrorist organisations such as Al-Qaeda and ISIS in the region necessitates continuous vigilance and a proactive approach. The UAE has focused on developing comprehensive counter-terrorism strategies and capabilities through defence Emiratisation. This includes establishing advanced intelligence networks, cyber and information warfare capabilities, modernised special forces units, and investment in research and development to counter emerging terrorism threats.

The UAE has also extended its efforts beyond its borders by actively participating in international counter-terrorism collaborations and initiatives to address the root causes of terrorism and promote regional stability.

The UAE's defence Emiratisation efforts are also influenced by the evolving dynamics within the Gulf Cooperation Council (GCC). The organisation has traditionally relied on collective defence arrangements and alliances with external powers to ensure regional security. However, recent geopolitical shifts and disagreements have necessitated a greater emphasis on self-sufficiency. Recognising the need for autonomy and a diversified defence industry, the UAE aims to reduce dependency on external actors for its defence needs. By promoting technological innovation, research and development, and local defence industry capabilities, the UAE seeks to become a regional powerhouse and contribute to the collective security of the GCC. These efforts include establishing defence research centres, collaborating with international defence companies, fostering partnerships with regional allies, and promoting the growth of defence-industrial capabilities within the country.

In conclusion, regional security concerns profoundly shape the defence's emiratisation efforts of the UAE. The threats posed by Iran, instability in neighbouring countries, transnational terrorism, and changing dynamics within the GCC all highlight the imperative for self-reliance in defence. Through developing a local defence industry, the UAE aims to enhance its capabilities, reduce vulnerabilities, and actively contribute to regional security and stability. By focusing on maritime security, counter-terrorism measures, regional collaborations, and building local defence-industrial capabilities, the UAE is firmly committed to ensuring a secure future for itself and the nation and the region.

IV

National Security Implications

Defence Emiratisation has far-reaching national security implications beyond reducing dependencies on foreign suppliers. This extended chapter will delve deeper into the multifaceted aspects of defence Emiratisation. It will explore how they contribute to the UAE's strategic autonomy, resilience to geopolitical shifts, and national security.

A. Economic Diversification and National Resilience:

One of the crucial benefits of defence Emiratisation is its contribution to economic diversification and national resilience. The UAE's commitment to developing a robust defence industry stimulates economic growth and creates job opportunities. By attracting foreign investments, the defence sector generates revenue. It fosters the transfer of knowledge and technology, contributing to the overall development of various industries.

Furthermore, a sophisticated defence ecosystem promotes technological innovation, research and development, and knowledge transfer. Through collaborative efforts between defence companies, universities, and research institutions, the UAE can nurture a highly skilled workforce and foster a culture of entrepreneurship. This builds resilience in the face of economic challenges and enhances the country's overall national security by reducing reliance on a single industry, such as oil and gas.

B. *Technological Advancements and Military Capability:*

Local defence industries enable nations to acquire advanced technologies, develop cutting-edge military capabilities, and maintain technological superiority. The UAE's focus on research and development programmes allows it to enhance its defence systems, innovate new technologies, and pioneer advancements in aerospace, cyber defence, artificial intelligence, and unmanned systems.

By investing in research and development, the UAE can effectively push the boundaries of military capabilities and address emerging threats. It can leverage technological advancements to enhance surveillance capabilities, improve command and control systems, and optimise the performance of defence equipment and vehicles. These technological advancements not only strengthen the UAE's military effectiveness but also contribute to the stability and security of the region.

Moreover, defence Emiratisation fosters domestic defence manufacturing and production capabilities, enabling the UAE to customise defence equipment and systems according to its unique operational requirements. This customisation enhances the effectiveness of defence operations and missions, improves interoperability between military units, and strengthens the overall capability and readiness of the armed forces. With local defence manufacturing facilities, the UAE can promptly upgrade, repair, and maintain its defence equipment without relying on foreign support, bolstering its self-reliance and military preparedness.

C. Research and Development Collaboration and International Cooperation:

While defence emiratisation promotes self-sufficiency, it encourages international collaboration in research and development projects. The UAE recognises the value of knowledge sharing and cooperation with global defence industry leaders, universities, research institutions, and defence equipment suppliers. Engaging in joint research and development initiatives allows the UAE to access state-of-the-art technologies, leverage external expertise, and acquire new capabilities quickly.

Strategic partnerships and collaborations with international defence companies facilitate technology transfer and the exchange of best practices. By learning from established defence industry players, the UAE can align its defence processes and standards with global norms, ensuring its defence sector remains at the forefront of technological advancements. These collaborations enhance the UAE's defence capabilities and contribute to regional and international security as the UAE becomes a trusted partner in defence innovation and technology.

D. Defence Export Opportunities and Soft Power Projection:

A successful defence Emiratisation strategy can transform the UAE into a significant player in the global defence market. By developing advanced defence systems and capabilities domestically, the UAE can position itself as a reliable exporter of defence equipment, technology, and services. This expands the UAE's economic influence and creates opportunities for building strong defence partnerships worldwide, strengthening diplomatic ties, and projecting its soft power internationally.

Strategic defence exports contribute to the national economy, generate revenue, and create jobs. They also reinforce the UAE's reputation and credibility as a reliable and technologically advanced defence partner, bolstering its regional influence and driving its national security objectives forward. Defence exports also foster diplomatic and military relationships with recipient nations, allowing the UAE to contribute to global security and significantly shape international defence frameworks.

In conclusion, defence Emiratisation in the UAE is a multifaceted endeavour with profound national security implications. It reduces dependencies on foreign suppliers, drives economic diversification, promotes technological advancements, strengthens military capabilities, fosters international collaboration, and presents defence export opportunities. The UAE's commitment to defence Emiratisation lays the foundation for a secure and self-reliant defence ecosystem that contributes to national security and regional stability.

A. Reduced Dependencies on Foreign Suppliers

One of the primary motivations for defence Emiratisation in the UAE is to reduce its heavy reliance on foreign suppliers for military equipment and technology. The UAE has relied heavily on imports to meet its defence requirements. This reliance on foreign suppliers has provided the country access to advanced weaponry and capabilities. Still, it has also made it vulnerable to supply chain disruptions, geopolitical shifts, and the whims of foreign suppliers.

The UAE's pursuit of a self-sufficient defence industry stems from a desire to exercise greater control over its defence capabilities. Relying on imports means subjecting national security to other nations' political considerations and interests. The UAE has embarked on developing its local defence industry to minimise these vulnerabilities and ensure a secure and sustainable supply of military equipment.

Reducing dependencies on foreign suppliers brings several advantages to the UAE. First, it gives the country greater control over its defence capabilities. By diversifying its defence suppliers domestically, the UAE can avoid external influences that might compromise its ability to protect its national interests. This additional control and autonomy allow the UAE to respond swiftly and effectively to emerging security challenges, irrespective of geopolitical developments or potential international restrictions on arms sales.

Moreover, reducing dependencies on foreign suppliers contributes to developing a diversified defence ecosystem within the UAE. By nurturing domestic defence industries, the country can foster collaboration between various sectors, such as academia, research institutes, and private enterprises. This collaboration promotes knowledge exchange, encourages innovation, and stimulates technological advancements. It also allows for integrating disciplines, from engineering and materials science to computer science and artificial intelligence, to create cutting-edge defence technologies tailored to the UAE's unique requirements and circumstances.

Developing domestic defence industries also contributes to economic growth and job creation within the UAE. Instead of spending large amounts of money on importing defence equipment and technology, the country can redirect its resources towards building domestic capabilities. This shift can lead to the development of a robust defence industrial base, which generates employment opportunities for skilled workers. Additionally, by producing defence equipment domestically, the UAE can potentially export its products and generate revenue, further boosting its economy.

Furthermore, reducing dependencies on foreign suppliers enhances the UAE's national security. By having control over the entire defence supply chain, the country ensures the availability of critical military equipment during times of crisis or international tensions. It reduces the risks associated with disruptions in the global supply chain, sanctions, embargoes, or political disagreements that may arise with foreign suppliers. This increased autonomy enables the UAE to maintain the readiness of its armed forces and effectively respond to emerging security threats.

Strategically reducing dependencies on foreign suppliers also contributes to the resilience and sustainability of the UAE's defence capabilities. The country can establish long-term partnerships with local manufacturers, enhance technology transfer, and foster local innovation by developing its domestic defence industry. These efforts allow the UAE to continuously upgrade its defence capabilities, adapt to emerging threats, and maintain a competitive edge in the region.

Furthermore, Emiratisation efforts provide opportunities for the UAE to develop its defence research and development (R&D) capabilities. By investing in R&D, the country can cultivate a culture of innovation and create cutting-edge military technologies tailored to its specific needs. This R&D focus promotes scientific advancements, attracts highly skilled researchers, and encourages collaboration with international defence firms, academia, and research organisations. By building a robust R&D infrastructure, the UAE can stay at the forefront of technological advancements, shaping the future of its defence capabilities.

In conclusion, reducing dependencies on foreign suppliers is critical to defence Emiratisation in the UAE. By developing its defence industry, the country aims to enhance its national security, achieve greater autonomy, bolster its economy, ensure the sustainability of its defence capabilities, and establish a diversified defence ecosystem. The UAE's pursuit of defence independence positions it as a self-reliant and technologically advanced nation capable of addressing emerging security challenges while maintaining control over its defence capabilities.

B. Enhancing Strategic Autonomy

As the United Arab Emirates (UAE) embarks on its journey towards defence Emiratisation, one of the key motivations is to enhance its strategic autonomy. Strategic autonomy refers to a nation's ability to plan and execute its defence policies independently without relying heavily on external actors. It allows a country to shape its destiny, safeguard national interests, and assert its influence in regional and international affairs.

Historically, the UAE has relied heavily on foreign defence suppliers for its military hardware and software needs. While this has ensured access to advanced technology, it has also posed challenges regarding flexibility, political dependencies, and potential vulnerabilities. Recognising the drawbacks of this dependence, the UAE has developed a comprehensive strategy for defence Emiratisation to achieve greater self-reliance and control over its defence capabilities.

By prioritising defence Emiratisation, the UAE aims to reduce its reliance on foreign suppliers and develop a robust local defence industry to meet its specific requirements. This pursuit of technological self-sufficiency allows the country to tailor its defence capabilities precisely to its unique security needs.

The UAE faces a complex security environment with territorial disputes, extremism, and regional rivalries. By developing domestic defence technologies and systems, the UAE can align them with its specific geopolitical circumstances and regional security challenges, enhancing the effectiveness and efficiency of defence operations.

Furthermore, defence Emiratisation contributes to the UAE's technological prowess and economic diversification. The country can nurture a pool of local expertise and talent by fostering innovation, research, and development in the defence sector. This benefits the defence industry and has broader economic and social implications. A strong defence industry can serve as a catalyst for the development of a knowledge-based economy, attracting foreign investment and creating high-skilled jobs. Developing local technologies can also have spillover effects, benefitting other sectors such as healthcare, telecommunications, and transportation. This diversification of the economy reduces dependency on oil and strengthens overall resilience, ensuring sustainable growth and prosperity.

Moreover, enhancing strategic autonomy through defence Emiratisation reduces the UAE's vulnerabilities to external influences and geopolitical shifts. Depending on foreign defence suppliers expose a country to risks such as political instability, economic sanctions, or changes in international alliances. The UAE can insulate itself from these uncertainties by developing its local defence industry and retaining control over its procurement processes. This ensures that external factors beyond its control do not compromise the UAE's national security interests. Furthermore, having a robust local defence industry enhances the UAE's credibility and influence in international relations. It strengthens the country's position as a reliable and capable partner, allowing it to negotiate from a place of strength and actively contribute to regional security initiatives, peacekeeping missions, and humanitarian operations.

The UAE must focus on several key areas to achieve defence Emiratisation and enhance strategic autonomy. Firstly, investing in research and development is crucial to drive innovation and technological advancement. Collaborations with leading academic institutions and international defence partners can provide access to knowledge exchange, cutting-edge technologies, and expertise. Moreover, attracting and retaining talented individuals in science, technology, engineering, and mathematics (STEM) fields is vital to building a skilled workforce capable of spearheading local defence projects.

Secondly, the UAE must foster cooperation between government entities, military branches, and the private sector. A whole-of-government and whole-of-society approach is needed to ensure seamless collaboration, knowledge sharing, and resource allocation. Encouraging public-private partnerships, supporting local defence manufacturers, and providing financial incentives can incentivise the growth of the local defence industry. Creating a favourable regulatory environment, streamlining procurement processes, and promoting intellectual property rights protection will further enhance the attractiveness of investing in the UAE's defence sector.

Furthermore, the UAE should actively engage in international defence exhibitions, conferences, and forums to showcase its defence capabilities and establish strategic partnerships. Collaborating with like-minded countries in research, development, and production can open doors to shared expertise, cost-sharing, and joint defence projects. Such partnerships enhance the UAE's technological capabilities and expand its defence export potential. The UAE can bolster its economy and strengthen its global influence by becoming a net exporter of local defence technologies.

In conclusion, the UAE's commitment to defence Emiratisation and pursuing strategic autonomy is a significant step towards securing its sovereignty, national security, and economic prosperity.

By reducing reliance on foreign defence suppliers, tailoring defence capabilities to specific security needs, fostering technological innovation, and building a robust local defence industry, the UAE strengthens its position in the regional and international spheres.

As the UAE progresses toward defence Emiratisation, it ensures its security. It contributes to global efforts to address emerging security challenges and maintain peace and stability. Through its strategic autonomy, the UAE becomes a reliable partner and a progressive force, harnessing its capabilities to shape a more secure and prosperous future for itself and its allies.

C. Resilience to Geopolitical Shifts

In a rapidly changing global geopolitical landscape, the United Arab Emirates' (UAE) pursuit of defence Emiratisation is crucial in ensuring resilience and adaptability to potential shifts. By reducing dependency on foreign defence suppliers, the country seeks to safeguard its national security interests and enhance its ability to navigate the complex dynamics of international relations.

One of the primary reasons for focusing on defence Emiratisation is to mitigate the risks associated with reliance on foreign countries for critical military equipment and technology. Geopolitical shifts, such as changes in alliances, fluctuations in international relations, or the imposition of arms embargoes, can disrupt the flow of defence supplies and pose significant challenges to a nation's security. By developing its defence capabilities, the UAE aims to establish a self-sufficient defence industry capable of sustaining its military requirements even in geopolitical uncertainty.

The UAE has embraced a multifaceted approach encompassing various strategic initiatives and partnerships to achieve defence Emiratisation. Central to this endeavour is creating a solid domestic defence industrial base, which involves collaboration with international defence companies to gain access to advanced technologies and knowledge transfer.

These partnerships allow the UAE to acquire cutting-edge defence systems and enable the transfer of expertise, helping build the country's local research and development capabilities.

In addition to seeking external collaborations, the UAE has made significant investments in developing its human capital to support the growth of the defence industry. Recognising the importance of innovation and a skilled workforce, the country has implemented initiatives like the UAE's Science, Technology, and Innovation (STI) Policy. This policy aims to foster an environment conducive to research and development, attract global experts, and promote entrepreneurship in defence technologies. Establishing specialised educational institutions, research centres, and innovation hubs further accelerates the cultivation of local talent and the creation of a skilled workforce in the defence sector.

Furthermore, defence Emiratisation grants the UAE greater control over its defence needs, allowing it to align its capabilities with national security objectives. This enhanced autonomy ensures that the country is not bound by external factors that may limit its ability to respond effectively to emerging security threats or regional challenges. The UAE can maintain flexibility and agility in adapting to geopolitical shifts without relying on external powers for their defence needs by possessing a local industry.

Resilience to geopolitical shifts also extends beyond military capabilities. As the UAE boasts a diversified and robust defence industry, it can effectively weather political changes and potentially contribute to stabilising the regional security environment. The ability to produce and export defence technologies strengthen economic ties and fosters diplomatic relationships with other nations. The UAE's defence emiratisation efforts can thus have positive spill-over effects in helping maintain stability in the Gulf region and exerting influence on international relations.

Moreover, defence Emiratisation aligns closely with the UAE's broader national agenda, emphasising diversified economic development and sustainable growth. Investing in defence Emiratisation, the country aims to foster technological innovation, boost research and development capabilities, and stimulate job creation across various sectors. This strategic approach helps build a knowledge-based economy, reduces reliance on oil revenues, and enhances the resilience of the UAE's overall socio-economic fabric. Besides, the UAE's pursuit of defence Emiratisation aligns with its long-term vision for the country as outlined in strategies like Vision 2021 and the UAE Centennial 2071. These national frameworks emphasise the importance of building a knowledge-based economy, investing in research and development, and cultivating a skilled workforce. By developing a local defence industry, the UAE enhances its national security. It advances its goals of economic diversification, technological advancement, and sustainable growth.

The UAE's commitment to defence Emiratisation has already yielded significant results. The country has made notable achievements in developing its military hardware, ranging from advanced fighter jets and armoured vehicles to naval vessels and missile systems. The UAE produces these defence systems domestically by reducing its dependence on foreign suppliers. It enhances its capability to customise and adapt these technologies to meet specific operational requirements.

In conclusion, resilience to geopolitical shifts is paramount for the UAE as it pursues defence Emiratisation. By reducing reliance on foreign suppliers, the country aims to safeguard its national security interests, enhance its autonomy, and ensure its ability to adapt effectively to the ever-changing dynamics of the international landscape. Developing a self-sufficient defence industry through partnerships, human capital development, and a focus on economic diversification ensures that the UAE can overcome future challenges, contribute to the stability of the wider region, and advance its broader national agenda.

V

Impact on National Defence Strategies

Reduced Dependency on Foreign Suppliers

One of the critical impacts of defence Emiratisation is the reduced dependency on foreign suppliers, thereby strengthening the UAE's national security. Historically, the UAE relied heavily on defence imports, which posed potential vulnerabilities. This reliance on foreign suppliers made the country susceptible to disruptions in the supply chain, such as export restrictions, political conflicts, or changes in international dynamics. However, the country's strategic shift towards developing local defence capabilities has significantly reduced this dependency, enhancing its self-reliance and overall defence posture.

By manufacturing defence equipment domestically, the UAE has gained greater control over its defence procurement. This control ensures the availability of critical military equipment and technology. It allows the UAE to secure its supply lines and mitigate potential delays caused by external factors. In times of crisis or conflict, the UAE can access and mobilise its local defence capabilities without relying on foreign suppliers, thus reducing the risk of supply chain disruptions that could threaten national security.

Moreover, defence Emiratisation enables the UAE to engage in technology transfer agreements with foreign partners. The country can access advanced defence technologies and knowledge through these agreements, which can be adapted and incorporated into its local defence systems. This facilitates the exchange of expertise and fosters technological innovation within the UAE's defence industry. By collaborating with international partners, the UAE can further enhance its local capabilities while reducing its reliance on specific countries or alliances, thus diversifying its defence relationships and strengthening its position in the global defence market.

Strategic Autonomy

Defence Emiratisation plays a crucial role in enhancing the UAE's strategic autonomy. By developing local defence capabilities, the country can control its decision-making processes and avoid dependence on external suppliers. This autonomy enables the UAE to align its defence strategies with its specific national security objectives, supporting its ability to respond effectively to emerging security challenges.

Furthermore, strategic autonomy in defence procurement strengthens the UAE's bargaining position in international defence partnerships and collaborations. By developing local capabilities, the country can negotiate from a place of strength, attracting potential partners to engage in joint ventures, cooperative research, and development programmes. This enhances the UAE's defence capabilities and diversifies its defence relationships. By reducing its overreliance on any single country or alliance, the UAE can navigate geopolitical shifts more effectively and ensure a steady supply of defence technologies and support even in changing international dynamics.

Resilience in Geopolitical Shifts

Defence Emiratisation contributes to the resilience of the UAE's defence sector, particularly in the face of geopolitical shifts. As global dynamics evolve, alliances and partnerships may change, and access to certain defence technologies or support may be restricted. The UAE's investment in local defence capabilities mitigates these risks by ensuring it can sustain its needs even during uncertainty or changes in the international security landscape.

Moreover, defence Emiratisation enables the UAE to become a potential defence exporter and a source of defence technology for other countries. By building advanced local defence capabilities and establishing a robust defence industrial base, the UAE can offer its expertise and capabilities to interested partner nations. This not only generates economic opportunities for the UAE but also strengthens its diplomatic ties and increases its soft power projection on the global stage. The ability to export local defence technologies establishes the UAE as a reliable partner in the defence industry, further bolstering its position in the international defence market.

Evolution of Military Doctrines

Developing and integrating local defence technologies require the evolution of military doctrines and strategies in the UAE. As the country incorporates its local capabilities into its defence strategies, military principles must be revised to optimise the utilisation of these technologies effectively. This includes adapting to the unique characteristics of local defence systems, ensuring interoperability with existing foreign equipment used by the UAE's armed forces, and maximising the effectiveness of these capabilities.

Integrating local defence technologies necessitates developing new operational concepts, tactics, and procedures to fully exploit these systems' capabilities. It also requires updating existing training programmes to ensure that personnel are well-versed in using and maintaining these local systems. By aligning military doctrines with the advances made in defence Emiratisation, the UAE can maximise its defence capabilities, optimise resource allocation, and effectively address emerging security challenges in a rapidly changing world.

Regional Defence Cooperation

Defence Emiratisation also has implications for regional military cooperation in the UAE. As the country strengthens its local defence capabilities, it can share its expertise and collaborate with neighbouring countries in the Gulf region. This cooperation can enhance regional security and foster stronger defence alliances, ultimately contributing to collective security within the area.

The UAE can serve as a hub for defence industry cooperation in the Gulf region, promoting the exchange of defence technologies, joint training exercises, and collaboration among regional partners. By leveraging its local defence capabilities, the UAE can take a more proactive role in supporting the defence needs of neighbouring countries and contribute to their defence Emiratisation efforts. This cooperation enhances regional security and strengthens the UAE's influence as a reliable and capable defence partner, encouraging stability and cooperation in the Gulf region.

In conclusion, defence Emiratisation significantly and multifacetedly impacts the UAE's national defence strategies. By reducing dependence on foreign suppliers, enhancing strategic autonomy, adapting military doctrines, and fostering regional defence cooperation, the UAE positions itself as a stronger player in the defence arena. Developing and integrating local defence technologies have strengthened the country's capabilities and contributed to regional security dynamics. The UAE's defence strategies will continue to adapt and evolve to maximise the benefits of defence Emiratisation while effectively addressing emerging security challenges in an ever-changing global landscape.

A. Reconfiguration of Defence Policies

In the quest for defence Emiratisation, a significant aspect that requires attention is the reconfiguration of defence policies. As the UAE strives to build its defence capabilities, redefining its national security and defence approach becomes essential. This chapter delves deeper into the critical elements of this reconfiguration process. It explores the implications it holds for the future.

1. SHIFTING FROM RELIANCE ON FOREIGN DEFENCE IMPORTS:

Reconfiguring defence policies involves a fundamental shift from relying on imports to focusing on local development and production. This shift necessitates a comprehensive reassessment of procurement strategies, including identifying critical defence technologies and systems that can be locally developed or sourced. It requires a thorough understanding of the country's defence requirements, strategic objectives, and the potential risks and vulnerabilities of relying on foreign suppliers. By prioritising the domestic industry, the UAE enhances its capability to respond swiftly to emerging threats, limits the exposure to external dependencies, and promotes self-sufficiency within the defence sector.

Proactive measures must be taken to achieve this shift, such as establishing strategic partnerships with foreign defence manufacturers to leverage their expertise while gradually transitioning knowledge and technology to local entities. The UAE should also invest in research and development capabilities to enhance its technological prowess and reduce dependence on foreign innovations. By fostering collaboration between the defence industry and academic institutions, the UAE can create an ecosystem that nurtures innovation, encourages technology transfer, and builds a skilled workforce adept at developing and producing local defence systems.

2. SETTING AMBITIOUS OBJECTIVES AND TARGETS:

Reconfiguring defence policies also entails setting clear objectives and targets for defence Emiratisation. This involves defining ambitious goals for the percentage of domestically produced defence equipment and technologies used by the armed forces. These goals should be determined through a comprehensive analysis of the country's defence needs, industrial capabilities, and the feasibility of developing or sourcing specific technologies. A robust target-setting process helps establish a sense of direction. It serves as a motivating factor for all stakeholders involved in the defence Emiratisation process.

To ensure the achievement of these objectives, the UAE can adopt a phased approach that gradually increases the percentage of domestically produced defence equipment over time. This strategy allows for a smooth transition, facilitates the development of local capabilities, and ensures the availability of critical defence technologies when needed. It is essential to periodically review and update these targets to align with technological advancements, emerging threats, and the overall development and growth of the local defence industry.

3. DEVELOPING LEGAL AND REGULATORY FRAMEWORKS:

The reconfiguration of defence policies necessitates the development of appropriate legal and regulatory frameworks that facilitate the growth of the local defence industry. This includes enacting laws encouraging investment in defence research and development (R&D), protecting intellectual property rights, and establishing quality control and product certification mechanisms. A practical legal and regulatory framework ensures transparency, promotes fair competition and protects national security interests. It also provides clarity and stability for both domestic and foreign investors, fostering confidence in the local defence industry.

The UAE can establish specialised agencies or departments overseeing defence procurement, export controls, and intellectual property protection. These entities can work closely with defence industry stakeholders, international partners, and regulatory bodies to ensure compliance and create an environment conducive to innovation, investment, and the sustainable growth of the local defence sector. At the same time, the UAE should actively participate in international forums and treaties that govern defence trade and technology transfer to garner support and influence global standards that facilitate its defence Emiratisation efforts.

4. HUMAN RESOURCE CAPACITY BUILDING:

Another crucial aspect of reconfiguring defence policies is the need for human resource capacity building. The UAE must invest in building a skilled workforce capable of conducting research, design, and manufacturing activities related to defence Emiratisation. This requires collaboration between academic institutions, vocational training centres, and defence industry players to develop specialised education and training programmes.

By equipping individuals with the necessary skills and knowledge, the UAE enhances its ability to sustain the growth and development of the local defence industry, fostering innovation and technological advancement.

The UAE should prioritise developing education and training programmes tailored to the defence sector's needs, focusing on engineering, advanced manufacturing, cybersecurity, and systems integration. Engaging international defence institutions and experts through partnerships and exchange programmes can further enrich the talent pool and expose UAE professionals to global best practices. Additionally, providing attractive incentives, scholarships, and sponsorships for students pursuing defence-related careers encourages a steady influx of talent into the industry, fostering long-term sustainability and expertise in developing local defence capabilities.

5. FORGING STRATEGIC PARTNERSHIPS AND COLLABORATIONS:

Reconfiguring defence policies involves forging strategic partnerships and collaborations at national and international levels. Through partnerships with foreign defence companies, the UAE can leverage their expertise and knowledge to accelerate the growth of its domestic defence industry. These partnerships can take different forms, including joint ventures, technology transfers, and collaborative research and development projects. Collaborations with other countries in the region can also lead to joint manufacturing initiatives, cost-sharing, and sharing of best practices. Such partnerships and alliances facilitate the transfer of technology and know-how while promoting the national interest of all involved parties.

The UAE can explore opportunities for collaboration with countries that have established local defence industries, enabling knowledge transfer and joint development of defence capabilities. Participating in international defence exhibitions, conferences, and forums fosters networking, knowledge exchange, and potential partnerships. Establishing defence innovation hubs or clusters within the UAE can serve as platforms for collaboration, attracting local and foreign companies to work together, access shared resources, and drive technological advancements in defence Emiratisation.

In conclusion, the process of defence Emiratisation in the UAE necessitates reconfiguring defence policies across various dimensions. Shifting from reliance on foreign defence imports, setting ambitious objectives, developing legal frameworks, investing in human resource capacity building, and forging strategic partnerships are all critical elements of this reconfiguration process. The UAE lays the foundation for sustained growth and self-reliance in the defence sector by comprehensively redefining defence policies. This, in turn, leads to enhanced national security and strategic autonomy.

B. Adaptation to Changing Geopolitical Dynamics

As the UAE embarks on its journey of defence Emiratisation, it becomes crucial to delve deeper into the challenges and opportunities presented by changing geopolitical dynamics. Adapting to these evolving geopolitical landscapes requires comprehensive analysis and strategic decision-making. This chapter explores the multifaceted aspects of adaptation, providing an in-depth understanding of the UAE's defence industry within the framework of shifting alliances, security priorities, regional conflicts, geopolitical risks, enhancing diplomatic relations, and multilateral cooperation.

1. UNDERSTANDING SHIFTING ALLIANCES:

a. Historical alliances and their changing nature:

The UAE's defence industry must acknowledge the historical alliances that have shaped the region while recognising its fluid nature. Historical relationships may evolve due to shifting geopolitical interests, emerging threats, or changing economic dynamics. Understanding these changes is essential for effectively leveraging alliances.

The UAE's long-standing alliance with the United States has been a pillar of its defence strategy. However, recent geopolitical shifts, such as the U.S.'s changing priorities and the emergence of new regional powers, necessitate a reassessment of the robustness and reliability of this alliance. Concurrently, the UAE has been strengthening diplomatic and economic ties with other global powers, such as China and Russia, opening up new avenues for defence collaboration and regional influence.

b. Regional power dynamics and emerging threats:

The UAE should closely monitor regional power dynamics to identify opportunities and challenges. Analysing the evolving roles of neighbouring countries and emerging threats such as terrorism, cyber-attacks, and asymmetric warfare will inform the defence Emiratisation strategy and resource allocation.

The UAE's immediate neighbourhood is witnessing significant transformations in power dynamics. The Iran-Saudi Arabia rivalry, the Yemen conflict, and the regional actors' evolving relationships pose complex challenges. Turkey's expanding influence, Russia's growing involvement, and China's economic investments in the region further contribute to the changing geopolitical landscape. By monitoring these dynamics, the UAE can determine how much it can rely on traditional allies and explore opportunities for diversifying partnerships.

c. The role of defence Emiratisation in adapting to realignments:

Defence Emiratisation empowers the UAE to adapt to realigned alliances by reducing reliance on external defence suppliers. The UAE can ensure its self-sufficiency and flexibility in response to changing geopolitical dynamics by developing local defence capabilities. The UAE's defence Emiratisation strategy is a proactive step towards adapting to changing alliances. By fostering local defence manufacturing, research and development, and advanced technological capabilities, the UAE aims to reduce its dependency on traditional suppliers and become more self-reliant.

This approach enhances the UAE's sovereignty and strategic autonomy and positions it as a credible partner in multinational defence collaborations.

2. EVALUATING SECURITY PRIORITIES:

a. Identifying critical national security concerns:
Understanding the UAE's key security concerns is crucial to inform defence Emiratisation efforts. This involves a comprehensive analysis of internal and external threats, including regional conflicts, territorial disputes, terrorism, and non-traditional security challenges such as climate change and cybersecurity.

The UAE's security priorities encompass diverse challenges. Internally, maintaining internal stability, combating extremism, and safeguarding social cohesion are crucial. Externally, ensuring the security of vital sea lanes, protecting critical infrastructure, and addressing regional conflicts like those in Yemen and Syria are crucial concerns. Moreover, emerging threats in cyberspace, the space domain, and artificial intelligence add complexity to the security landscape, necessitating continuous adaptation.

b. Analysing regional security challenges and trends:

Assessing regional security challenges and trends is essential for aligning defence Emiratisation goals with the evolving security environment. Consideration should be given to conflict zones, emerging geopolitical hotspots, maritime security risks, and the proliferation of advanced military technologies.

The Middle East is grappling with a multitude of security challenges. Ongoing conflicts in Syria, Iraq, and Yemen have destabilised the region and created power vacuums that non-state actors exploit.

Regionally, tensions over territorial disputes and resource competition persist, with conflicts such as the Qatar blockade and the Iran-Saudi Arabia rivalry exacerbating instability. Furthermore, the proliferation of advanced military technologies and the increasing sophistication of threats present new challenges that the UAE must address through defence Emiratisation.

c. Assessing the role of defence Emiratisation in addressing security needs:

Defence Emiratisation enables the UAE to enhance its defence capabilities, address security needs, and safeguard national interests. By developing a robust defence industry, the UAE can address specific security concerns and reduce vulnerabilities stemming from external dependencies.

The UAE seeks to enhance its capacity to meet evolving security needs through defence Emiratisation. By focusing on research and development, knowledge transfer, technology acquisition, and local production, the UAE aspires to develop advanced defence capabilities that address emerging threats. This process allows for customising defence solutions to align with specific security needs, ensuring optimal operational effectiveness and resilience across multiple domains.

3. THE INFLUENCE OF GLOBAL POWER PLAYERS:

a. Impact of significant powers' policies on regional stability:

The UAE should observe and understand the policies of major global powers, recognising their influence on regional stability. Examining the involvement of the United States, Russia, and China in the Middle East will help shape the UAE's defence Emiratisation strategy.

The engagement of significant powers in the Middle East has far-reaching implications for regional stability. The United States, despite showing signs of selective disengagement from the region, remains a key security partner for the UAE.

Understanding the dynamics of U.S. policies, such as the emphasis on burden-sharing and the prioritisation of their Indo-Pacific strategy, is essential when reevaluating the UAE's defence dependencies.

Russian presence and assertiveness in the Middle East, particularly in Syria, underscores the need to account for their regional influence. Understanding Russia's strategic objectives and growing arms exports to the region will inform the UAE's defence Emiratisation strategy.

Similarly, China's increasing economic investments and expanding military footprint have implications for the UAE's long-term defence planning, necessitating careful analysis of its intentions and strategic importance.

b. The role of defence Emiratisation in gaining strategic autonomy:

Defence Emiratisation allows the UAE to assert greater strategic independence by reducing reliance on foreign military equipment and technologies. Enhancing self-sufficiency helps offset potential risks associated with external influences and strengthens the UAE's ability to protect its sovereignty.

Strategic autonomy is a core goal of the UAE's defence Emiratisation efforts. The UAE can minimise potential vulnerabilities from changing geopolitical dynamics by reducing reliance on external defence suppliers. Self-sufficiency in advanced defence capabilities allows the UAE to safeguard its sovereignty, make independent strategic choices, and react effectively to emerging security threats. This pursuit of strategic autonomy also strengthens the UAE's position as a reliable partner in collaborative defence initiatives.

c. Opportunities for collaboration and competition with global players:

Collaboration opportunities with global players should be explored as the UAE develops its defence industry. Engaging in joint research and development projects, technology transfers, and knowledge exchange can facilitate the growth of the defence sector while fostering international collaboration.

Simultaneously, healthy competition should be encouraged to drive innovation and maintain a resilient defence sector.

Collaboration with global defence players presents opportunities for the UAE to access advanced technologies, tap into global expertise, and foster knowledge-sharing. Partnering with international defence companies, research institutions, and defence technology hubs can accelerate the development of local capabilities, enhance research and development capabilities, and foster innovation.

Collaborative projects, such as joint ventures and technology-sharing agreements, can expand the UAE's defence industry and create a foundation for long-term partnerships. Engaging in joint research and development efforts with global players allows the UAE to leverage their expertise and access cutting-edge technologies, reducing development time and cost.

While collaboration is beneficial, healthy competition should also be encouraged to drive innovation and maintain a resilient defence sector. A competitive environment fosters the development of advanced defence technologies and encourages the UAE's defence industry to improve and stay at the forefront of global innovation continuously.

4. MANAGING GEOPOLITICAL RISKS:

a. Understanding geopolitical risks and their implications:

Geopolitical risks, such as regional conflicts, terrorism, and economic instability, can significantly impact the security landscape and influence defence Emiratisation efforts. Analysing these risks and their implications ensures that the UAE's defence industry is well-equipped to adapt and respond effectively. A high level of geopolitical risks characterises the Middle East.

Ongoing conflicts and territorial disputes in the region can escalate and directly impact the UAE's security environment.

Terrorism, both conventional and cyber-based, poses a persistent threat that requires continuous adaptation and agile defence capabilities. Economic instability, caused by fluctuating oil prices and global economic trends, can also affect defence Emiratisation efforts. Understanding these risks allows the UAE to develop strategies that mitigate vulnerabilities and ensure the resilience of its defence industry.

b. Building resilience through diversification and contingency planning:

The UAE should embrace diversification and implement contingency planning to manage geopolitical risks effectively. Diversifying defence partnerships, suppliers, and supply chains reduces dependence on single sources and increases resilience. Developing contingency plans enables the UAE to respond swiftly and effectively to unforeseen disruptions and security challenges. Diversification of defence partnerships and suppliers is crucial to building resilience against geopolitical risks. By expanding partnerships with multiple countries, the UAE can reduce vulnerability to disruptions caused by shifting alliances or regional conflicts. Diversifying supply chains and sources of critical defence equipment and technologies reduces dependency on specific countries, mitigating risks associated with geopolitical tensions.

Contingency planning enables the UAE to respond swiftly and effectively to unforeseen disruptions. The UAE can ensure the continuity of its defence capabilities even in challenging circumstances by assessing potential scenarios, developing response measures, and establishing alternative supply routes. Contingency planning allows the UAE to adapt its defence Emiratisation strategy based on evolving geopolitical risks.

c. The role of defence Emiratisation in managing geopolitical risks:

Defence Emiratisation is crucial in managing geopolitical risks by reducing vulnerability to external factors and increasing self-sufficiency.

By developing a robust defence industry, the UAE can address security challenges and maintain operational capabilities despite changing alliances or disruptions in the global supply chain. The UAE reduces dependence on external suppliers through defence Emiratisation, mitigating risks associated with geopolitical tensions or disruptions in the global defence market. Developing local defence capabilities enables the UAE to maintain operational readiness and protect its sovereignty, even when faced with security challenges from regional conflicts or evolving alliances.

Additionally, defence Emiratisation enhances the UAE's ability to respond to emerging threats, such as cyber-attacks or asymmetric warfare. By developing advanced technologies and capabilities, the UAE can stay ahead of evolving risks and adapt its defence posture accordingly, ensuring the resilience of its national security.

5. STRENGTHENING DIPLOMATIC RELATIONS AND MULTILATERAL COOPERATION:

a. Leveraging defence Emiratisation to enhance diplomatic relations:
Defence Emiratisation can catalyse and enhance diplomatic relations with key regional and international partners. The UAE can be a reliable partner by developing local defence capabilities and fostering trust and cooperation in defence and security. The UAE's defence Emiratisation efforts can contribute to strengthening diplomatic relations through defence cooperation agreements, joint military exercises, and technology transfers. As the UAE develops advanced defence capabilities, it can offer collaborative opportunities to its international partners, reinforcing bilateral and multilateral ties. This can lead to deepened strategic partnerships and enhanced cooperation in areas beyond defence, such as trade and investment.

Moreover, the UAE can enhance its credibility and autonomy in diplomatic negotiations by reducing its dependence on foreign defence suppliers.

The UAE's ability to meet its defence needs and contribute to regional security through its local capabilities adds weight to its diplomatic initiatives. It strengthens its position as a global player.

b. Multilateral cooperation in defence and security:

Multilateral cooperation is crucial in addressing regional security challenges and responding to evolving geopolitical dynamics. Engaging in multilateral forums, such as regional defence alliances or international security organisations, allows the UAE to collaborate with like-minded countries, pool resources, and collectively address shared security concerns.

The UAE can leverage its defence Emiratisation efforts to enhance multilateral cooperation in defence and security. By showcasing its technological advancements, research and development capabilities, and defence manufacturing capacity, the UAE can contribute to collaborative defence initiatives. This includes joint training programs, information-sharing mechanisms, and coordinated efforts to address shared security threats.

Participating in multilateral forums allows the UAE to voice its perspectives on regional security challenges and influence policy discussions. By actively engaging in regional and international talks, the UAE can shape the discourse on defence and security priorities, contributing to the stability and prosperity of the region.

c. Balancing national interests and multilateral obligations:

While engaging in multilateral cooperation, the UAE must maintain a delicate balance between its national interests and multilateral commitments. Defence Emiratisation should not compromise the UAE's ability to protect its sovereignty, pursue its national security objectives, or make independent strategic decisions. Maintaining a balance between national interests and multilateral obligations requires careful strategic planning and clear articulation of priorities.

The UAE should ensure that its defence Emiratisation strategy aligns with its long-term security goals and does not compromise its ability to respond to emerging threats effectively. At the same time, the UAE should actively participate in multilateral initiatives to contribute to regional stability and foster cooperative security arrangements.

CONCLUSION:

Adaptation to changing geopolitical dynamics is a complex and ongoing process that requires comprehensive analysis, strategic decision-making, and continuous evaluation. The UAE's defence Emiratisation efforts are crucial in this process, enabling the country to adapt to shifting alliances, address evolving security priorities, manage geopolitical risks, enhance diplomatic relations, and engage in multilateral cooperation.

The UAE can develop a defence Emiratisation strategy that aligns with the evolving geopolitical landscape by understanding the historical context of alliances, analysing regional power dynamics, and evaluating security concerns. Strengthening diplomatic relations and engaging in multilateral cooperation further enhance the UAE's position as a reliable partner and active participant in regional and international security initiatives.

Through defence Emiratisation, the UAE can enhance its strategic autonomy, reduce vulnerabilities, and ensure the resilience of its defence capabilities. Building a robust defence industry encompassing research and development, local production, and technological advancement allows the UAE to adapt to changing geopolitical dynamics and effectively address security challenges.

As the UAE's defence industry evolves and adapts, it should remain agile and responsive to the constantly changing geopolitical environment.

Regular reassessment, flexibility in strategy, and continuous innovation will protect the UAE's long-term defence and security interests amidst shifting geopolitical dynamics.

C. Alignment with National Security Objectives

Economic factors or geopolitical considerations do not merely drive defence Emiratisation in the United Arab Emirates (UAE). It is a strategic imperative that aligns closely with the country's national security objectives. By developing a robust defence industry within its borders, the UAE aims to enhance its defensive capabilities and ensure the security of its citizens in an increasingly complex and volatile global landscape.

One of the primary goals of defence Emiratisation is to reduce reliance on foreign suppliers for critical defence equipment, technologies, and services. This objective stems from recognising that dependence on external sources poses inherent risks, especially during geopolitical volatility or shifts in international alliances. Relying heavily on imports results in vulnerable supply chains and leaves the country susceptible to potential embargoes or sanctions that may disrupt the consistent flow of essential defence capabilities. By cultivating local defence capabilities, the UAE seeks to take control of its defence procurement processes and reduce the vulnerabilities associated with relying on foreign entities.

Furthermore, defence Emiratisation aligns with the UAE's ambitions to become a leading technological powerhouse. Investing in local defence capabilities not only bolsters its national defence but also stimulates technological advancements and innovation across various sectors of the economy. The defence industry acts as a catalyst, driving research and development activities, creating high-skilled jobs, fostering collaboration between academia and industry, and attracting foreign investment in advanced technologies. By nurturing local expertise in research, development, and production of advanced defence systems, the UAE aims to propel its domestic defence industry and position itself at the forefront of cutting-edge technologies, such as artificial intelligence, cybersecurity, and autonomous systems. This alignment with national security objectives extends beyond self-sufficiency; it establishes the UAE as a powerhouse for defence innovation and opens doors for international collaboration in technological advancements.

Moreover, the alignment with national security objectives encompasses regional considerations as well. The UAE recognises the need to play an active and influential role in shaping the Gulf region's security dynamics and balance of power. By strengthening its defence industry, the UAE can contribute to regional stability, deter potential threats, and establish itself as a reliable security partner. Collaborative defence projects, knowledge-sharing platforms, joint military exercises, and defence diplomacy initiatives promote mutual trust and understanding among neighbouring countries. By actively participating in regional security efforts, the UAE enhances its security while safeguarding the broader interests of the Gulf Cooperation Council (GCC) and contributing to its overall stability.

Regarding defence strategies, Emiratisation aligns with the UAE's goal to create a more agile and adaptive military force. Developing and manufacturing defence equipment locally enables the armed forces to effectively tailor their capabilities to suit specific operational requirements and counter emerging threats.

The ability to rapidly adapt and respond to evolving challenges enhances the overall effectiveness and readiness of the national defence forces.

Locally produced defence systems can be designed with end-users input, allowing for customised solutions that address unique operational requirements.

Additionally, domestic production capabilities enable quicker response times in times of urgency or conflict, reducing dependence on international supply chains and potentially increasing the operational tempo of the armed forces. This alignment enables the UAE to maintain an edge in modern warfare, maximising its military's operational efficiency and combat effectiveness.

The alignment of defence Emiratisation with national security objectives is also reflected in the allocation of resources. The UAE government recognises the need to prioritise defence spending to achieve the desired outcomes in terms of national security. Investing in developing and expanding the local defence industry ensures sufficient financial resources are directed towards building a self-reliant defence ecosystem. This alignment bolsters the UAE's national security, generates jobs, fosters economic growth, and encourages technological advancements, ultimately benefiting the nation. The financial benefits stemming from defence Emiratisation extend beyond the immediate defence sector, creating ripple effects across various industries and contributing to overall prosperity.

In conclusion, aligning defence Emiratisation with national security objectives is a strategic imperative for the UAE. By reducing dependence on foreign suppliers, enhancing technological capabilities, contributing to regional stability, and aligning with specific defence objectives, the UAE aims to secure its autonomy, resilience, and readiness to defend its national interests.

This comprehensive approach is fundamental to strengthening the UAE's position as a critical player in the global defence landscape while ensuring the safety and well-being of its people. By harnessing the potential of the defence industry, the UAE is charting a path towards long-term security, sustainable economic growth, and the technological prowess necessary to navigate an ever-evolving security environment.

VI

Evolution of Military Doctrines

As the UAE continues its journey towards defence Emiratisation, the evolution of military doctrines becomes critical. With the integration of local technologies and the development of localised defence capabilities, there are significant implications for how the national armed forces operate and strategise.

A. Integration of Local Technologies

The shift towards defence Emiratisation necessitates the integration of local technologies into the UAE's military doctrines. This involves developing and incorporating advanced weaponry systems, surveillance and reconnaissance capabilities, communication networks, and cyber defence mechanisms. By embracing homegrown technologies, the national armed forces can enhance operational efficiency and effectiveness, promoting a previously unattainable self-reliance.

Integrating local technologies strengthens the UAE's military defence and creates a positive ripple effect across the nation's economy. The development of defence capabilities largely relies on cutting-edge technological advancements, which result in increased research and development activities, job creation, and skill acquisition. This fosters a thriving defence-industrial complex, enabling the UAE to build a robust technological base and create a competitive advantage in the global defence market.

Furthermore, integrating local technologies gives the UAE flexibility in addressing evolving threats. By actively participating in the research and development of defence technologies, the nation can respond to emerging challenges more rapidly. The ability to adapt and innovate in real-time ensures that the national armed forces remain at the forefront of defence readiness, maintaining a deterrent posture and ensuring the security of the UAE and its citizens.

B. Adaptation to Localised Defence Capabilities

The evolution of military doctrines also entails adapting to the localised defence capabilities developed through Emiratisation. This involves training and equipping the armed forces to effectively utilise these capabilities in various scenarios, ranging from conventional warfare to asymmetric threats. By honing their skills and familiarising themselves with locally developed defence systems, UAE's military personnel can maximise the effectiveness of these capabilities, further enhancing the country's overall defence posture.

In addition to enhancing operational effectiveness, adapting to localised defence capabilities promotes a sense of national pride and ownership. As the armed forces increasingly rely on locally developed technologies, a collective responsibility arises to protect and nurture the nation's defence industry. This sense of ownership is a strong motivator for soldiers and military leaders, instilling a higher level of dedication and commitment to the UAE's defence.

Moreover, the adaptation to localised defence capabilities fosters a culture of innovation within the armed forces. As military personnel engage with these systems, they gain valuable insights that can refine and advance future Emiratisation efforts. This feedback loop between operators and developers ensures continuous improvement, enabling the UAE to remain at the cutting edge of defence technology.

C. Implications for Regional Military Cooperation

The evolution of military doctrines due to defence Emiratisation has broader implications for regional military cooperation in the Gulf region. As the UAE enhances its local capabilities, it opens avenues for collaboration with neighbouring countries and the potential sharing of knowledge, resources, and expertise. This can foster greater regional integration and coordination, ultimately contributing to a more robust collective security framework.

The UAE can leverage its defence Emiratisation efforts to position itself as a reliable regional partner. The country can build trust and strengthen military alliances by showcasing its advanced technologies and defence capabilities. Multilateral military exercises, joint training programmes, and information-sharing initiatives can further enhance collaboration among Gulf countries, creating a united front against common security challenges.

Furthermore, by highlighting its success in defence Emiratisation, the UAE can become a hub for international defence cooperation and partnerships. Global defence players may seek to collaborate with the UAE in research and development, manufacturing, and technology transfer, further bolstering the nation's defence industry and contributing to its economic diversification goals.

In the context of regional military cooperation, the evolution of military doctrines due to defence Emiratisation can also lead to the establishment of joint defence initiatives. With its localised capabilities, the UAE can lead in developing frameworks for joint defence projects, such as multinational task forces or shared defence infrastructure. These endeavours would contribute to enhanced interoperability among regional militaries and strengthen the overall defence capabilities of the Gulf region.

In sum, the evolution of military doctrines in the UAE is integral to the defence Emiratisation process. With the integration of local technologies and the adaptation to localised defence capabilities, the national armed forces are well-placed to enhance their operational capabilities and contribute to regional security. Moreover, the evolution of military doctrines presents opportunities for increased regional military cooperation, paving the way for a more integrated and secure Gulf region. Additionally, the UAE's defence Emiratisation efforts have the potential to boost the nation's economy, create jobs, and establish the country as a global centre for defence innovation and collaboration.

A. Integration of Local Technologies

In pursuing defence Emiratisation, the United Arab Emirates (UAE) has strongly emphasised integrating local technologies into its national defence system. Acknowledging the critical role of technological autonomy in achieving self-reliance, the country has made significant strides in developing and incorporating a robust local technological base.

1. TECHNOLOGICAL ADVANCEMENTS AND RESEARCH

The UAE recognises that technological advancements form the bedrock of a modern and capable defence system. Extensive investment has been made in research and development initiatives to foster innovation and drive technological progress. State-of-the-art research facilities equipped with cutting-edge technology and staffed by highly skilled scientists and engineers have been established throughout the country.

Collaboration with renowned international research institutions has further bolstered the UAE's technological capabilities. Through knowledge sharing and joint projects, the country remains at the forefront of emerging technologies, enabling the development of advanced defence systems.

In addition, the UAE actively participates in conferences, symposiums, and exhibitions to showcase its local technological advancements and foster collaborations with global defence partners.

2. DEVELOPMENT OF LOCAL DEFENCE TECHNOLOGIES

A vital aspect of the UAE's defence Emiratisation strategy is the development of local defence technologies across various domains. By cultivating homegrown expertise and fostering a culture of innovation, the country has successfully produced a wide array of cutting-edge defence technologies.

The UAE has achieved significant milestones in developing local capabilities within the aerospace sector. The country's aerospace companies have designed and manufactured advanced unmanned aerial systems (UAS), aircraft, and related systems, showcasing their ability to create, develop, and integrate sophisticated aerospace platforms for military and civilian applications. These technologies include autonomous drone systems, surveillance and reconnaissance aircraft, and high-altitude long-endurance vehicles.

In addition to aerospace technologies, the UAE's defence industry has also focused on producing land-based systems. Developing local armoured vehicles, weapon systems, and communication technologies has strengthened the country's ground defence capabilities. Advanced capabilities include armoured personnel carriers with enhanced mobility and survivability features, precision-guided munitions, and secure communication systems for reliable battlefield connectivity.

Furthermore, the UAE has prioritised the development of cyber-security technologies to protect critical infrastructure and combat cyber threats. Advanced systems for network defence, secure communications, and data encryption have been developed to safeguard national security interests in the digital domain. These technologies are crucial in securing sensitive military networks, preventing cyber espionage, and responding effectively to cyberattacks.

3. INTEGRATION OF LOCAL TECHNOLOGIES

Successful Emiratisation requires the seamless integration of local technologies within the larger defence ecosystem. The UAE has prioritised interoperability, ensuring local systems and platforms can effectively work with existing defence infrastructure.

Integration efforts involve extensive planning, coordination, and standardisation to optimise the performance and effectiveness of local technologies in real-world operational scenarios. The UAE's defence industry collaborates closely with the armed forces during integration, conducting rigorous testing and evaluation to ensure that systems meet the highest operational and safety standards.

International collaboration also plays a crucial role in integration processes. The UAE actively engages with global defence partners to exchange expertise, learn best practices, and adopt international standards. This approach ensures that local technologies are not only advanced but also readily compatible with international defence systems, fostering interoperability and cooperation on a global scale.

The UAE has established dedicated centres for systems integration and interoperability testing to facilitate integration. These centres bring together experts from various disciplines to evaluate and harmonise local technologies, ensuring seamless communication and cooperation between systems and platforms.

4. ROLE OF PUBLIC-PRIVATE PARTNERSHIPS

The UAE has actively promoted public-private partnerships (PPPs) in defence technology development to expedite the integration of local technologies into the defence sector. Collaborations between the defence industry, academia, and research institutions have facilitated the exchange of knowledge, expertise, and resources, leading to accelerated advancements and integration of local technologies.

PPPs have enabled the commercialisation of defence technologies, opening new avenues for economic growth and innovation.

The UAE has encouraged international defence companies to establish joint ventures and participate in technology transfer activities by attracting foreign direct investment and fostering a favourable business environment. This has strengthened the local defence industry and diversified the country's economic landscape.

The UAE government also actively supports small and medium-sized enterprises (SMEs) in the defence sector through various initiatives. These initiatives provide financial assistance, mentorship programmes, and access to advanced research and development facilities, enabling SMEs to play a significant role in developing and integrating local defence technologies. Such support fosters a vibrant ecosystem of local defence technology providers, further boosting the country's defence Emiratisation efforts.

5. TRAINING AND SKILL DEVELOPMENT

The full potential of local technologies can only be realised when personnel possess the necessary knowledge and skills to operate, maintain, and innovate these systems effectively. Recognising this, the UAE has implemented extensive training and skill development programmes for defence personnel and relevant industries.

Training programmes focus on building technical competencies and operational expertise. Personnel receive comprehensive training on local defence technologies' operation, maintenance, repair, and upgrade processes. Simulations and practical exercises enhance operational readiness, ensuring seamless integration and optimal utilisation of these technologies.

The UAE also places great importance on human capital development to sustain the integration and utilisation of local technologies in the long run. Scholarships, research grants, and mentorship programmes are provided to nurture local talent, fostering a strong pool of skilled engineers and scientists who will continue to drive technological advancements in defence.

Additionally, knowledge transfer programmes allow collaboration between experienced foreign experts and UAE engineers, promoting the transfer of technical know-how and fostering a culture of continuous learning and innovation.

6. CHALLENGES AND FUTURE PROSPECTS

As with any ambitious endeavour, challenges lie on the path towards complete integration of local technologies. Technological advancements are necessary to keep pace with evolving threats and maintain a cutting-edge defence capability. This requires sustained investment in research and development and building strong partnerships with global technology leaders.

Another crucial challenge is addressing cybersecurity concerns amid an increasingly interconnected world. Robust cybersecurity measures must be developed and integrated into local technologies to protect against potential threats and vulnerabilities, ensuring the integrity and confidentiality of sensitive defence information. The UAE continues enhancing its cybersecurity research capabilities, developing advanced solutions to tackle emerging cybersecurity challenges.

The UAE's commitment to defence Emiratisation and the integration of local technologies remains unwavering. The country's dedication to technological advancement, innovation, and collaboration positions it favourably for the future. By striving towards complete self-reliance, the UAE aims to enhance its defence capabilities, promote national security, and contribute to the growth of a knowledge-based economy. The UAE aims to consolidate its position as a leading global player in local defence technologies through continued investment, research, collaboration, and skill development.

B. Adaptation to Localised Defence Capabilities

In the process of defence Emiratisation, one crucial aspect is the adaptation of national defence strategies to meet the capabilities of the local defence industry. Integrating localised defence capabilities gives the UAE a unique advantage in tailoring its military doctrines to suit its specific needs and challenges. However, this requires a comprehensive evaluation of existing military principles, strategic planning, and coordination efforts to maximise the potential of localised defence capabilities.

1. ALIGNING OPERATIONAL STRATEGIES WITH LOCAL TECHNOLOGIES

To align operational strategies with local technologies, the UAE's armed forces need to thoroughly understand the capabilities and limitations of the homegrown defence systems and platforms. This requires comprehensive assessments and evaluations of the local assets to identify their strengths and weaknesses. By gaining insight into these aspects, the armed forces can develop operational tactics and strategies that effectively leverage the localised defence capabilities while mitigating potential risks.

Collaboration between the defence industry and the armed forces is crucial in aligning operational strategies with local technologies. The defence industry possesses valuable knowledge about the capabilities of locally developed defence systems and platforms. Sharing this information with the military enables them to incorporate such capabilities into operational planning and decision-making. The armed forces' feedback, in turn, aids the defence industry in refining and improving their technologies, fostering innovation and growth.

2. ENHANCING INTEROPERABILITY WITH LEGACY SYSTEMS

One of the primary challenges in the adaptation to localised defence capabilities is ensuring interoperability and compatibility with existing defence systems and equipment procured from foreign sources. Integration of new technologies without disrupting established operations requires meticulous planning and coordination.

To address this challenge, the UAE's armed forces must establish effective protocols and frameworks for interoperability. This entails conducting comprehensive compatibility tests to identify potential issues and developing strategies to overcome them. Standardising communication protocols and data formats is also crucial for seamless integration. Training programmes should ensure that personnel are well-versed in operating both localised and legacy systems, enabling them to switch between platforms efficiently. Additionally, retrofitting or upgrading legacy systems can help align them with emerging technologies, promoting interoperability without compromising effectiveness.

3. INVESTING IN RESEARCH AND DEVELOPMENT

Sustained investment in research and development (R&D) is critical for the long-term success of localised defence capabilities. The defence industry must foster a culture of innovation, continuously pushing the boundaries of technological advancement to remain at the forefront of defence capabilities. Collaborative efforts with academic institutions think tanks and international defence players can facilitate knowledge-sharing and leverage diverse expertise, accelerating the development of localised defence technologies.

To establish a foundation for local R&D excellence, the UAE should establish robust research institutions focused on defence technologies. These institutions should have cutting-edge laboratories, testing facilities, and simulation capabilities. Attracting top talent worldwide through competitive incentives and scholarships will contribute to a culture of innovation and intellectual growth. Long-term strategic partnerships with international defence players can provide access to advanced technologies, collaborative funding opportunities, and knowledge-sharing platforms that foster the development of localised defence capabilities.

4. ECONOMIC IMPLICATIONS AND JOB CREATION

Beyond meeting national security objectives, adapting to localised defence capabilities has significant economic implications. The development of the defence sector contributes to economic growth and diversification, creating employment opportunities for skilled professionals. The localised defence industry supports the growth of high-tech manufacturing. It promotes the development of associated sectors such as engineering, research, and software development.

To fully harness the economic potential of localised defence capabilities, the UAE can encourage knowledge transfer and skill development through partnerships with international defence players. Such collaborations can provide opportunities for the UAE's workforce to gain exposure to global best practices and cutting-edge technologies. By fostering collaboration and knowledge-sharing, the UAE can enhance the capabilities of its workforce, stimulating innovation and entrepreneurship within the defence sector.

Furthermore, strategic partnerships can attract foreign direct investment and facilitate technology transfer, bolstering the growth of localised defence capabilities and strengthening the national economy. The UAE's commitment to fostering a robust defence industry ecosystem can be a magnet for foreign investors seeking to capitalise on the country's expertise and potential. This investment inflow further stimulates job creation and promotes the development of a skilled workforce, leading to a sustainable and technologically advanced defence-industrial complex.

In conclusion, adapting to localised defence capabilities is a multifaceted process that requires careful planning, collaboration, and integration efforts. By aligning operational strategies with the powers of local technologies, the UAE's armed forces can maximise their effectiveness in protecting national security interests. Overcoming challenges related to interoperability with legacy systems and fostering a culture of continuous research and development is critical to the success of localised defence capabilities. Moreover, the economic implications of defence Emiratisation should not be overlooked, as the growth of the defence sector leads to job creation and economic diversification.

C. Implications for Regional Military Cooperation

Regional military cooperation is crucial in enhancing collective security and stability in the Gulf region. The process of defence Emiratisation in the United Arab Emirates (UAE) has significant implications for regional military cooperation and collaboration. This chapter explores the impact and opportunities of the UAE's efforts to strengthen its defence capabilities through local production.

First and foremost, defence Emiratisation allows the UAE to transfer its expertise and technological advancements to neighbouring countries in the region. As the UAE develops its local defence industry, it gains valuable knowledge and capabilities that can be shared through military training programmes, joint exercises, and collaborative research and development initiatives. This strengthens regional military cooperation by creating a more level playing field and fostering a sense of shared security.

Besides, defence Emiratisation enhances the UAE's credibility and influence within regional defence alliances. The UAE has become an attractive partner for other regional countries by developing advanced technologies and establishing a robust defence industrial base. This, in turn, strengthens the UAE's diplomatic ties and allows for deeper military collaboration, including joint operations, intelligence sharing, and joint defence planning. The UAE's enhanced capabilities also make it a valuable contributor to regional peacekeeping missions and humanitarian operations, further solidifying its position as a critical player in regional military cooperation.

In addition, defence Emiratisation promotes interoperability among regional armed forces. As the UAE develops and utilises its defence systems and technologies, neighbouring countries must align their defence capabilities and equipment with the UAE's standards to effectively collaborate. This alignment encourages standardised military practises and equipment interoperability, ultimately enhancing the effectiveness of regional defence operations. Improved interoperability facilitates joint training exercises, combined military operations, and the sharing of operational tactics and strategies, enabling regional forces to work seamlessly together in addressing shared security challenges.

Moreover, defence Emiratisation can potentially drive regional technological innovation and economic growth. The UAE's investment in local defence production creates jobs and fosters research and development, leading to advancements in defence technologies and capabilities. These technological advancements can subsequently be shared with regional partners, further driving innovation and elevating the overall defence capabilities of the Gulf region. Additionally, the growth of the defence industry contributes to economic diversification, reducing dependence on oil revenue and stimulating the development of a knowledge-based economy.

Furthermore, defence Emiratisation can lead to the emergence of regional defence alliances centred around shared defence industries as countries in the Gulf region develop their local defence capabilities, opportunities for strategic collaboration and resource sharing increase. Joint ventures, defence technology transfers, and collaborative production agreements can emerge, leading to a more integrated regional defence industry.

This strengthens regional military cooperation and offers economic advantages through economies of scale and cost-sharing opportunities. The shared investment in defence technologies and production facilities contributes to the growth of local defence industries, creating jobs and stimulating economic diversification in the region.

However, defence Emiratisation also presents challenges to regional military cooperation. It may create disparities in defence capabilities among regional partners, potentially leading to imbalances that must be addressed to ensure effective coordination and collaboration. Additionally, competition for defence contracts and market share among Gulf countries may strain relationships and require skilful diplomacy and negotiation to maintain regional unity. Transparency and open communication channels are crucial in mitigating such challenges and fostering trust among regional partners.

In conclusion, defence Emiratisation in the UAE has significant implications for regional military cooperation in the Gulf region. The UAE's advancements in local defence production create opportunities for knowledge sharing, strengthen diplomatic ties, promote interoperability, drive technological innovation, and foster the emergence of regional defence alliances. While challenges exist, such as potential disparities and competition, the potential benefits make defence Emiratisation a valuable pathway for enhancing regional security, stability, technological advancement, and economic growth through cooperation in defence industries.

VII

Performance of the National Armed Forces

The performance of the national armed forces in the United Arab Emirates (UAE) has experienced a significant boost through defence Emiratisation. This strategic shift towards developing domestic defence technologies has resulted in the acquisition of state-of-the-art military capabilities tailored to meet the specific needs and challenges faced by the UAE.

A. Enhanced Capabilities through Emiratisation

The Emiratisation of defence technologies has proven pivotal in strengthening the armed forces' capabilities in the UAE. The UAE has successfully acquired advanced military equipment and systems that align with its unique security requirements by focusing on developing domestic defence industries. This shift has allowed the armed forces to move away from relying solely on generic solutions provided by foreign suppliers and instead tailor their capabilities to address local challenges effectively.

The UAE's defence industry has attained notable operational advancements through a robust commitment to research and development. This process involves continuous experimentation, innovation, and refinement to create cutting-edge technologies. The armed forces now possess various capabilities encompassing aerospace, naval systems, land-based defence technologies, cyber warfare, and beyond.

In the aerospace domain, the UAE has achieved remarkable milestones. The country developed and successfully deployed the "Project Dolphin," a local drone technology that enhances aerial surveillance capabilities. This system showcases the UAE's expertise in autonomous unmanned aerial vehicles (UAVs), which play a vital role in reconnaissance, surveillance, and target acquisition. The UAE's aerospace advancements extend to developing local fighter aircraft, with projects such as "Project Saham" pushing the boundaries of technological prowess.

The naval systems have also witnessed substantial growth. The UAE's defence industry has invested in developing next-generation warships and naval vessels capable of operating in coastal and deep-sea environments. These vessels are equipped with cutting-edge sensors, defensive countermeasures, and offensive capabilities, ensuring the protection of coastal waters and the ability to project power beyond the region when necessary.

On land, the UAE's national armed forces have focused on developing advanced military vehicles and artillery systems to defend its borders and support ground operations. Developing local armoured vehicles, such as the "Liwa" family of mine-resistant ambush-protected vehicles, has enhanced protection for personnel deployed in high-risk zones. Additionally, the UAE has pioneered the creation of self-propelled artillery systems, incorporating advanced fire control systems and autonomous functionalities to bolster its artillery capabilities.

The armed forces have also prioritised the development of cyber warfare capabilities to defend against evolving digital threats. The deployment of advanced cybersecurity systems and robust intelligence capabilities have helped protect critical infrastructure and sensitive military information from cyberattacks. The UAE's national armed forces have fostered collaborations with international cybersecurity experts to strengthen their defensive posture against cyber threats as part of their ongoing commitment to Emiratisation.

B. Challenges and Opportunities

While defence Emiratisation has brought about substantial improvements in the capabilities of the national armed forces, it has not been without challenges. Developing local defence technologies requires significant investments in research and development, establishing specialised facilities, and cultivating a skilled workforce. These endeavours can strain the defence budget and require a long-term commitment to sustain.

To address these challenges, the UAE government has prioritised investment in education and vocational training programmes to develop a pool of skilled professionals capable of supporting the defence industry. Universities and research institutions across the UAE have also established collaboration agreements with international defence organisations and academic institutions, allowing for knowledge exchange and the transfer of expertise.

Moreover, the UAE's defence industry is relatively young compared to established defence industries in other countries.

This youthfulness can result in gaps in knowledge and experience, which must be addressed through partnerships with international defence companies or consultants. However, these challenges also present knowledge transfer and collaboration opportunities, allowing the UAE's defence industry to accelerate its growth and enhance its capabilities through shared expertise.

The UAE government has taken proactive steps to foster collaboration with international defence companies, drawing on their established know-how and experience. These partnerships have enabled the exchange of best practices and technology transfer, providing the UAE's defence industry with valuable insights and enhancing its capabilities. Additionally, international joint ventures have facilitated the establishment of local manufacturing facilities, creating job opportunities and promoting the growth of the UAE's defence ecosystem.

C. Comparative Analysis with Previous Import-Dependant Models

When evaluating the performance of the national armed forces before and after embracing defence Emiratisation, a clear shift in capabilities becomes evident. Historically, the UAE heavily relied on imports to fulfil its defence needs. While this approach allowed for the rapid acquisition of advanced military equipment, it also rendered the armed forces dependent on foreign suppliers, leaving them vulnerable to geopolitical considerations beyond their control.

In stark contrast, the shift towards defence Emiratisation has reduced the UAE's reliance on foreign suppliers and enhanced its control over defence capabilities. The armed forces can now respond promptly to any threats or challenges without being constrained by external factors. Furthermore, developing local defence technologies has empowered the UAE to customise military assets to address specific regional security concerns, providing a distinct advantage over adversaries.

The strategic trajectory of defence Emiratisation has elevated the performance of the national armed forces in the UAE. Improved capabilities and access to advanced military equipment have made the armed forces more self-reliant and adept at efficiently addressing regional security challenges. While challenges persist, the opportunities for growth and collaboration in the defence industry present a promising future for the UAE's national defence. This continued focus on defence Emiratisation will undoubtedly further strengthen the UAE's position as a critical player in regional security and contribute to its sustained success in safeguarding national interests.

A. Enhanced Capabilities through Emiratisation

The successful implementation of defence Emiratisation in the UAE has led to significant advancements in the capabilities of the national armed forces, transforming the country into a regional leader in defence technologies and innovation. By investing in research, development, and production of local defence technologies, the UAE has achieved greater self-reliance, enhanced readiness, and strengthened its military capacity.

One of the critical benefits of defence Emiratisation is the ability to customise and adapt technologies to meet the specific requirements of the UAE's national defence strategy. This has allowed the country to develop defence systems tailored to its unique regional challenges, such as the vast desert landscape and the critical importance of maritime security. The UAE has created advanced surveillance and reconnaissance capabilities that optimise effectiveness in these environments by capitalising on its knowledge of the local terrain and operational needs.

In land warfare, the UAE has developed local armoured vehicles that excel in challenging desert conditions. These vehicles, equipped with advanced navigation systems, enhanced mobility, and superior firepower, provide a decisive edge during military operations. With climate-controlled cabins and innovative technologies combating sand and dust infiltration, the UAE's armoured vehicles ensure the safety and comfort of its personnel in extreme temperatures and harsh desert environments. Furthermore, integrating advanced communication systems and network-centric capabilities enhances coordination among units. It enables real-time data sharing and decision-making, improving the overall operational effectiveness of the armed forces.

In the maritime domain, the UAE's locally developed naval capabilities have propelled it to become a regional maritime power. The country's shipyards have successfully manufactured state-of-the-art naval vessels, including patrol boats, corvettes, and frigates. These vessels are designed to address the challenges faced in the Arabian Gulf, such as piracy, smuggling, and protecting vital maritime infrastructure. Equipped with cutting-edge radar systems, advanced weapon systems, and multi-mission capabilities, these local naval platforms enable the UAE to safeguard its territorial waters, secure strategic seaways, and project power across the region.

Its pursuit of advanced aerial capabilities further exemplifies the UAE's commitment to defence Emiratisation. The country has invested in developing and producing local unmanned aerial systems (UAS), also known as drones, which have proven instrumental in conducting surveillance, reconnaissance, and targeted strikes against terrorist organisations and other threats. These UAS are designed to operate seamlessly in the UAE's unique operational environment, with considerations for extreme temperatures, sandstorms, and long endurance missions. With its robust UAS capabilities, the UAE can gather effective intelligence, maintain situational awareness, and swiftly respond to emerging threats.

Furthermore, the UAE's Emiratisation efforts extend to cybersecurity and information warfare, recognising the need to safeguard critical infrastructure and combat ever-evolving cyber threats.

The country has established cybersecurity centres of excellence, which foster collaboration between government agencies, academia, and industry experts. By nurturing local talent in cybersecurity research, development, and implementation, the UAE has significantly strengthened its defence against cyber-attacks. Locally developed cybersecurity solutions, along with solid legislation and regulatory frameworks, ensure the protection of national systems, critical networks, and sensitive information, bolstering the country's overall resilience in the face of emerging cyber threats.

The journey toward defence Emiratisation has not been without its challenges. Developing a local defence industry requires substantial human capital, infrastructure, and technological research investments. The UAE has overcome these challenges by prioritising long-term planning, coordination, and collaboration between government agencies, military entities, and industry stakeholders. Establishing strategic partnerships with leading defence companies and centres of excellence worldwide has facilitated knowledge transfer, technology acquisition, and skill development. Moreover, by actively encouraging public-private partnerships and fostering an enabling environment for businesses, the UAE has attracted foreign direct investment, further stimulating its defence industry's growth and competitiveness.

In conclusion, the UAE's unwavering commitment to defence Emiratisation has propelled the nation to the forefront of regional defence capabilities and innovation.

By leveraging its unique operational context and fostering collaboration between sectors, the UAE has successfully harnessed its local defence industry to develop tailored solutions that address domestic challenges and align with its national defence strategy.

Whether it be the production of advanced armoured vehicles for land warfare, the manufacture of cutting-edge naval vessels for maritime security, the development of local UAS for aerial operations, or the establishment of robust cybersecurity systems for information protection, the UAE stands as a testament to the rewards that come with sustained investment in defence Emiratisation.

With a strategic vision, strong leadership, and unwavering commitment, the UAE inspires nations globally, demonstrating the benefits and capabilities that can be achieved through a comprehensive and well-executed Emiratisation strategy.

B. Challenges and Opportunities

The journey towards defence Emiratisation in the UAE has its fair share of challenges. Still, it also presents numerous opportunities for economic growth, security, and international recognition. As the nation progresses in developing its defence capabilities, it must navigate and overcome these challenges to fully realise the potential of this endeavour.

One of the primary challenges faced by the UAE lies in building a robust domestic defence industry from scratch. This involves establishing a comprehensive infrastructure for research and development, manufacturing, and maintenance of military equipment. Substantial investments in technology, facilities, and skilled workforce are necessary to achieve this goal. The UAE must set up institutions that prioritise defence research and development, collaborate with academia to foster innovation and provide efficient testing and evaluation facilities for emerging technologies.

Developing a skilled and specialised workforce is crucial for the success of Emiratisation efforts. The UAE must invest in vocational training programmes and educational initiatives that align with the requirements of the defence industry. This includes supporting technical colleges and universities that offer programmes in engineering, defence sciences, and related fields. Collaborative partnerships with international defence firms can further enhance these efforts by providing access to training programmes, internships, and knowledge-sharing platforms.

Amidst the pursuit of Emiratisation, the UAE faces the challenge of international competition. Established global defence suppliers have significant influence and established reputations, making it difficult for the UAE's nascent defence industry to compete on a level playing field. The UAE should actively seek collaborative partnerships and technology transfers with international defence firms to address this. By fostering beneficial relationships, the UAE can leverage established manufacturers' expertise and experiences while accelerating the development of local capabilities.

Another significant challenge is ensuring the sustainability and continuity of defence Emiratisation efforts. This requires establishing a long-term strategy that can withstand changes in government priorities and economic fluctuations. The UAE must develop a clear roadmap that outlines the milestones and targets of its defence Emiratisation plan. Robust governance structures and effective coordination among various stakeholders in the defence sector are essential for successful implementation and adaptation to emerging technologies and evolving security needs.

Despite these challenges, the UAE has numerous opportunities to exploit in its pursuit of defence Emiratisation. The nation's strategic geographic location and proximity to regional conflicts provide ample opportunities to test and refine domestic defence systems in real-world scenarios. The UAE can actively engage with its regional partners to shape collaborative defence initiatives and strengthen security alliances. Participating in regional defence efforts enhances the UAE's defence capabilities and fosters trust and strategic partnerships with neighbouring countries.

The UAE's existing partnerships with foreign defence firms also create opportunities for technology transfer and knowledge exchange, facilitating the accelerated development of local capabilities. By carefully selecting partners and negotiating appropriate technology-sharing agreements, the UAE can access cutting-edge defence technologies, methodologies, and best practices, which can be adapted to meet their unique requirements.

Moreover, defence Emiratisation presents immense economic opportunities for the UAE. The nation can create high-skilled jobs by establishing a robust domestic defence industry, attracting foreign direct investment, and promoting economic diversification. The defence sector can contribute to the nation's broader goal of reducing dependence on oil revenues and creating a knowledge-based economy. The UAE's success in developing advanced defence technologies and gaining expertise positions it as a potential supplier to other nations in need, further enhancing its economic prospects in the global defence market.

However, the UAE must address certain critical factors to capitalise on these opportunities. Fostering a culture of innovation within the defence industry is essential. This can be achieved by supporting research and development initiatives, incentivising collaboration between academia, industry, and the military, and integrating defence innovation clusters into the national innovation ecosystem.

Investing in research and development is another crucial aspect of building a sustainable defence industry. The UAE must allocate adequate resources towards funding research projects, creating testbeds for emerging technologies, and establishing centres of excellence that focus on specialised areas of defence technology.

Adequate intellectual property protection is paramount to attracting further investment and encouraging technological advancements.

The UAE must strengthen its intellectual property laws and enforce them rigorously to assure technology providers that their assets will be safeguarded.

In conclusion, pursuing defence Emiratisation in the UAE is multi-faceted, involving challenges and opportunities that require careful navigation. By developing a comprehensive strategy, investing in infrastructure and skilled workforce, fostering collaboration with international partners, and creating an enabling environment for innovation and research, the UAE can overcome these challenges and leverage the opportunities. This, in turn, will contribute towards the nation's economic growth, security, and recognition as a capable defence partner on the international stage.

C. Comparative Analysis with Previous Import-Dependant Models

In this chapter, we will conduct a detailed comparative analysis between the current defence industrialisation initiatives in the UAE and the previous import-dependent models. By exploring each approach's differences, strengths, weaknesses, and challenges, we can gain valuable insights into the transformation of the UAE's defence industry, which is reshaping its national security landscape.

The reliance on foreign defence suppliers in the UAE's past import-dependant models can be attributed to several factors. Firstly, limited domestic capabilities and expertise made it necessary for the country to procure advanced weaponry, technology, and military hardware from international sources. As a relatively young nation, the UAE required time to build its local defence industry. During this developmental phase, imported defence systems were crucial in ensuring readiness and operational effectiveness.

Another critical driver of import dependency was the UAE's strategic goal of acquiring state-of-the-art defence technologies and capabilities.

Recognising the importance of maintaining a technological advantage in an evolving security landscape, the UAE sought cutting-edge defence equipment from the best sources worldwide. The UAE aimed to deter potential threats by procuring advanced systems, enhancing operational capabilities, and projecting power regionally and globally.

Moreover, geopolitical considerations and strategic partnerships influenced the UAE's import-dependant models. Building relationships with crucial defence suppliers allowed the country to secure tailored military solutions and establish long-term collaboration on joint research, development, and training programmes. The UAE gained access to cutting-edge technology, knowledge transfer, and market influence by aligning itself with renowned defence industry leaders.

However, the import-dependant model had vulnerabilities and limitations, hindering the UAE's national security resilience. A primary concern was the potential for disruptions in the supply chain, which could occur due to political factors, embargoes, sanctions, or strained diplomatic relations. Such disorders could leave the UAE vulnerable to shortages in critical defence equipment, maintenance support, and spare parts, hindering its ability to respond effectively to emerging threats.

Additionally, reliance on foreign suppliers often meant limited control over developing, customising, and upgrading defence systems. The UAE relied on external sources for technical support, upgrades, and maintenance, which could lead to delays, increased costs, and potential limitations in systems' compatibility and interoperability. This dependence on foreign entities could compromise the UAE's sovereignty, flexibility, and ability to respond swiftly and independently to dynamic security challenges.

The current defence Emiratisation efforts in the UAE have aimed to address these vulnerabilities and build a robust and self-sufficient defence industry.

Significant progress has been made in developing local defence capabilities, establishing local research and development centres, and nurturing a culture of innovation, advanced manufacturing, and technology transfer. The UAE's vision of building a local defence industry has guided its national security doctrine, underlining the need for technological independence, self-reliance, and diversification.

The UAE has invested heavily in building domestic defence manufacturing infrastructure, attracting foreign expertise, and promoting knowledge transfer. It has focused on creating strategic alliances with international defence partners to gain access to cutting-edge technology and foster collaboration in research, development, and training. These partnerships provide opportunities for the UAE to enhance its local capabilities, leverage global advancements in defence technology, and ensure long-term sustainability and growth.

By reducing dependence on imports, the UAE has achieved more significant control over developing and customising defence systems, improving operational readiness, reliability, and maintenance capabilities. This shift has enhanced the country's national security resilience by reducing the risks associated with supply chain disruptions and ensuring continued access to critical defence equipment, technology, and expertise.

Furthermore, defence Emiratisation has stimulated economic growth and diversification in the UAE. The development of the domestic defence industry has created job opportunities, both directly in defence manufacturing and indirectly through the expansion of associated support industries. Investments in research and development have contributed to knowledge-based economies, fostering innovation and technological advancements in other sectors as well. This economic benefit has strengthened the UAE's financial base and increased its self-sufficiency in defence procurement, further bolstering national security.

Nonetheless, the transition to a domestically-driven defence industry has presented its challenges. Developing advanced defence technologies requires significant research, development, and infrastructure investment. Acquiring the necessary technological know-how and expertise can be time-consuming and resource-intensive. The UAE has addressed these challenges by emphasising collaboration with international defence establishments, facilitating technology transfers, and conducting joint research and development programmes. This approach has allowed the UAE to expedite its defence Emiratisation efforts.

Moreover, maintaining a balanced approach to defence procurement, leveraging locally developed capabilities and selective imports, remains crucial. While the UAE continues to strengthen its domestic defence industry, there are areas where specific technologies, components, or systems may still require collaboration with international partners. Strategic partnerships and joint ventures facilitate access to advanced defence technologies and enable the UAE to benefit from global research and development investments, thereby saving resources and time.

To optimise future development, the UAE must continuously evaluate and assess the effectiveness of its defence Emiratisation efforts. It is crucial to strike the right balance between self-reliance and strategic partnerships with global defence industry leaders to harness synergies and advancements in research and development. Additionally, establishing a robust export capability will enable the UAE's defence industry to contribute to international security and generate additional economic benefits.

In conclusion, the comparative analysis between the UAE's current defence industrialisation efforts and previous import-dependent models highlights the significant strides in building a self-sufficient defence industry.

The transition has enhanced the UAE's national security resilience by reducing dependence on foreign suppliers, ensuring access to critical defence equipment, and stimulating economic growth and diversification. By evaluating each approach's strengths, weaknesses, and challenges, the UAE can continue to refine its defence industry strategies and capitalise on its achievements to shape a secure and prosperous future.

VIII

National Defence Budgets

A. Economic Impacts of Defence Emiratisation

The process of defence Emiratisation has profound economic implications that reach far beyond national security. While the primary goal of defence Emiratisation is to enhance a country's self-sufficiency in defence capabilities, it also brings significant economic benefits. These benefits can be observed in both the short-term and long-term, as the Emiratisation process stimulates various sectors of the economy and contributes to overall economic growth.

In the short term, defence Emiratisation necessitates substantial investments in research and development, technological advancements, and establishing domestic defence industries. These investments often result in increased government spending, leading to a potential boost in the overall economy. Research and development initiatives require funding to support innovation, leading to advancements in defence technologies and related fields such as science, engineering, and manufacturing. This, in turn, creates job opportunities and drives economic growth through increased economic activity.

Furthermore, establishing domestic defence industries requires investment in infrastructure, such as production facilities and specialised equipment. This investment stimulates the construction industry and contributes to the growth of local manufacturing capabilities. As domestic defence industries grow, they create a ripple effect throughout the supply chain, supporting other sectors such as raw material providers, logistics companies, and service providers. This increased economic activity generates additional employment opportunities, further contributing to economic development.

However, the economic benefits of defence Emiratisation extend far beyond the short term. Developing local defence technologies and industries holds the potential for long-term economic diversification and resilience. By reducing reliance on foreign defence imports, countries like the UAE can redirect their defence budgets towards nurturing domestic industries, thus bolstering critical sectors of the economy. These sectors often include research and development, high-tech manufacturing, and advanced engineering, which foster innovation, attract foreign investment, and create high-value job opportunities.

Moreover, defence Emiratisation can act as a catalyst for broader economic diversification efforts. By developing local defence capabilities, countries can acquire knowledge, expertise, and technologies that have applications beyond defence. These spillover effects can lead to the creation of new industries, the commercialisation of defence technologies for civilian use, and the development of a highly skilled workforce. The growth of these industries enhances a country's economic competitiveness. It reduces dependence on a single sector, making the economy more resilient to external shocks and fluctuations.

B. Allocation of Resources

The successful implementation of defence Emiratisation relies on effectively allocating resources within national defence budgets. A strategic approach ensures that crucial defence capabilities, research and development initiatives, infrastructure, and human capital are adequately supported.

To achieve this, governments must prioritise the development of critical defence capabilities that address present and future security challenges. This may involve investing in cutting-edge technologies, such as artificial intelligence, cybersecurity, and autonomous systems, which have become increasingly relevant in modern security. Allocating resources to these areas enhances a country's defence capabilities, fosters innovation, and supports the growth of related industries.

Furthermore, investing in research and development is crucial to defence Emiratisation. Governments must allocate funds to support research institutions, collaborate with academia and industry, and encourage innovation. This investment not only drives technical advancements but also strengthens the knowledge base and expertise within the country. By nurturing a culture of innovation and creativity, governments can create a sustainable ecosystem that fosters the growth of local defence industries and supports economic diversification.

Infrastructure development is another critical component of resource allocation. Governments must invest in the construction of specialised defence production facilities, testing centres, and technology parks to support the growth of domestic industries. These investments create jobs in the construction sector and provide a dedicated space for research, development, and production. Additionally, infrastructure development initiatives can have ripple effects on other sectors by improving connectivity, logistics, and the overall business environment, promoting economic growth beyond the defence industry.

Lastly, the proper allocation of resources must also consider the cultivation of human capital. Governments must invest in education and training programmes to develop a highly skilled workforce capable of supporting local defence industries. This investment can range from funding research scholarships and grants to establishing specialised vocational training centres and promoting partnerships between academia and industry. By ensuring a continuous supply of skilled professionals, countries can effectively bridge the gap between defence requirements and human resources, driving the long-term growth and sustainability of the defence industry.

C. Cost-Benefit Analysis

Conducting a comprehensive cost-benefit analysis is pivotal in budgeting for defence Emiratisation. This analysis evaluates the costs associated with developing local defence technologies against the potential long-term benefits from an economic and security perspective.

In terms of costs, governments must consider the financial investments required and the time, effort, and expertise needed to develop local defence capabilities successfully. These costs include research and development expenses, infrastructure investments, and human capital development. Governments should also assess the risks and challenges associated with defence Emiratisation, such as delays, technological setbacks, and the need for extensive collaboration between various stakeholders.

On the other hand, the benefits of defence Emiratisation must be thoroughly evaluated. From an economic perspective, governments must assess the potential long-term financial impact of developing domestic defence industries. This involves considering the direct and indirect benefits, such as job creation, increased economic activity, and the attraction of foreign investment. Additionally, governments should examine the long-term cost savings resulting from reduced dependence on foreign defence imports. Countries can mitigate the expenses of purchasing, maintaining, and upgrading foreign defence systems by cultivating domestic defence industries. These cost savings can be redirected to other sectors, fuelling economic growth and diversification.

From a security perspective, the benefits of defence Emiratisation involve an enhanced national defence capability and a reduced reliance on external sources for critical defence technologies. A local defence industry provides countries with strategic autonomy, enabling them to safeguard their interests and respond effectively to rapidly evolving security challenges. Moreover, defence Emiratisation fosters the development of homegrown expertise, ensuring a self-sufficient defence sector that can adapt to changing security dynamics without being hampered by external dependencies.

In conclusion, defence Emiratisation has significant economic implications beyond national security. While short-term costs may be incurred during the initial stages of development, the long-term benefits can be transformative for the economy as a whole. The allocation of resources within defence budgets must be strategic, ensuring investments in essential defence capabilities, research and development, infrastructure, and human capital. Additionally, conducting a comprehensive cost-benefit analysis is imperative to evaluate defence Emiratisation's financial feasibility and potential economic and security gains. By navigating these considerations effectively, countries like the UAE can achieve self-sufficiency in defence while fuelling economic growth, fostering innovation, and increasing overall resilience.

A. Economic Impacts of Defence Emiratisation

The Emiratisation of defence in the UAE holds vast economic implications that extend beyond superficial benefits. By delving deeper into the financial impacts of this strategic approach, we can uncover many factors that shape the country's trajectory and long-term objectives.

1. Economic Diversification: The UAE recognises the importance of abandoning its overreliance on oil revenues and moving towards a knowledge-driven economy. Defence Emiratisation serves as a critical catalyst in this endeavour. By nurturing a domestic defence industry and creating new sectors, the country broadens its economic base, reduces vulnerability to oil price fluctuations, and fosters resilience in financial uncertainty. Moreover, the diversification of the economy minimises the risk of job losses and ensures sustainable growth.

The UAE government's Vision 2021 strategic plan aims to reduce the contribution of oil to the country's GDP from approximately 30% in 2021 to 20% by 2021. Defence Emiratisation plays a pivotal role in achieving this goal. The development of the domestic defence industry creates new economic sectors. It attracts foreign direct investment (FDI), promotes technology transfer and knowledge exchange, and stimulates innovation and entrepreneurship. These ripple effects contribute to a sustainable and diversified economy, reducing the nation's excessive dependence on hydrocarbon reserves.

2. Job Creation and Skill Development: Establishing domestic defence capabilities creates a skilled workforce and employment opportunities for UAE citizens. This, in turn, reduces unemployment rates and enhances labour productivity. The defence sector demands expertise from engineering and technology specialists to, project managers and logistics professionals. As the industry expands and evolves, it provides a platform for skill development and knowledge transfer, ultimately strengthening the human capital within the country.

To bridge the gap between workforce availability and industry demands, the UAE's government has implemented various initiatives. For instance, the UAE National Service Programme has been instrumental in cultivating talent by providing young Emiratis with military training, language skills, and leadership development opportunities. Moreover, partnerships between defence firms, educational institutions, and research centres have been formed to design specialised training programmes. These efforts ensure that the workforce possesses the necessary skills to contribute effectively to the defence industry and other sectors of the economy.

3. Enhanced National Security: Indigenising defence capabilities boost economic growth and strengthen national security. By reducing reliance on foreign defence equipment and technologies, the UAE gains greater control over its defence infrastructure, ensuring self-sufficiency and enhancing its strategic autonomy. This improved national security creates a stable and secure environment, attracting foreign investment and bolstering the overall economy.

Besides, developing a robust domestic defence industry enhances the UAE's capacity to address evolving security threats and adapt to geopolitical challenges.

The country can maintain an adequate defence posture by accessing advanced technologies, reducing vulnerabilities to supply chain disruptions, and streamlining procurement processes. This proactive approach to national security ensures the UAE's stability. It fosters confidence among foreign investors and trading partners, encouraging partnerships and boosting economic growth.

4. Technology Acquisition and Innovation: Developing a domestic defence industry allows the UAE to access advanced technologies through partnerships with international defence firms or foreign governments. This technology transfer not only enhances the defence sector but also contributes to advancements in other sectors of the economy. The acquired capabilities have spill-over effects, encouraging innovation, research and development, and the adoption of advanced technologies in aerospace, information technology, and telecommunications.

The UAE government has established dedicated research centres and innovation hubs in collaboration with defence industry leaders and academic institutions to promote innovation and technological advancement. These centres focus on cybersecurity, artificial intelligence, and autonomous systems, driving breakthroughs that benefit both defence and civilian applications. By fostering an innovation ecosystem, the UAE cultivates a competitive edge in emerging technologies, attracting international investment and generating economic opportunities beyond the defence sector.

5. Economic Multiplier Effect: The growth of the defence industry has a far-reaching impact on other sectors of the economy. As the defence sector expands, it stimulates demand for various goods and services, opening opportunities for local businesses and entrepreneurs to flourish. The defence ecosystem requires various supportive industries, including logistics, transport, manufacturing, and legal support.

This creates a multiplier effect, triggering economic activity, facilitating knowledge exchange, and fostering a vibrant business environment. The establishment of military supply chains, the construction of defence infrastructure, and the procurement of raw materials and components all contribute to local economic growth. Small and medium-sized enterprises (SMEs) play a crucial role in this ecosystem, providing specialised services and products, creating job opportunities, and enhancing competitiveness. The defence industry's demand for advanced technologies, software solutions, and cyber defence also stimulates innovation and entrepreneurship in the UAE's digital economy, fostering further economic diversification and growth.

6. Geopolitical Influence and Export Potential: A robust local defence industry positions the UAE as a significant player in the global defence market, enhancing its geopolitical influence while providing avenues for defence exports. Armed with local expertise, innovative capabilities, and advanced technologies, the UAE can potentially export defence-related products and services to other nations. This boosts revenues, strengthens diplomatic ties, and creates opportunities for strategic alliances.

The UAE's defence industry has been booming in exporting various products, including armoured vehicles, naval vessels, and unmanned aerial systems, creating new revenue streams. In addition to generating economic benefits, defence exports shape the country's foreign policy and strengthen relationships with strategic partners. The UAE's reputation as a reliable defence supplier has grown, enabling it to meet domestic requirements, compete globally, and support international peacekeeping efforts.

However, the Emiratisation of defence also presents challenges. Establishing a domestic defence industry requires substantial initial investments in research and development, infrastructure, and talent acquisition.

The process necessitates collaboration between the government, private sector, and educational institutions to build a self-sustaining ecosystem. Additionally, the industry must adapt to the ever-changing global market dynamics, ensuring continuous innovation, cost-effectiveness, and a competitive edge.

In conclusion, the economic impacts of defence Emiratisation in the UAE reach far beyond a simple diversification strategy. This approach creates employment opportunities, fosters skill development, strengthens national security, drives technology acquisition and innovation, generates economic multiplier effects, and projects the UAE as a significant player on the global stage. As the country strides towards building its domestic defence industry, it simultaneously lays the foundation for a resilient, diverse, and prosperous future economy.

B. Allocation of Resources

The process of allocating resources in the defence industry plays a crucial role in successfully implementing defence Emiratisation efforts. This chapter will explore the various factors and considerations determining how resources are allocated to developing local defence capabilities in the UAE.

1. Strategic Priorities:

a. National Security Objectives: Resources allocation must align with the country's national security objectives. This involves identifying key focus areas and setting strategic priorities to ensure resources are used effectively to meet defence and security needs. National security objectives may include safeguarding territorial integrity, maintaining regional stability, countering terrorism, securing critical infrastructure, and protecting national interests abroad.

b. Threat Assessment: A comprehensive assessment of potential threats helps determine resource allocation. This includes analysing current and future security challenges, both national and regional. Threat assessment involves studying geopolitical dynamics, assessing the military capabilities of potential adversaries, analysing emerging technologies, and identifying vulnerabilities that need to be addressed. By understanding the threats, resource allocation can be tailored to develop capabilities that effectively counter potential risks.

2. Defence Budget:

a. Funding Sources: The defence budget is the primary source for defence Emiratisation efforts. It is essential to identify the different funding sources, such as government allocations, revenue from natural resources, and international partnerships or collaborations. Additionally, exploring avenues for private sector investments and venture capital can enhance the available financial resources for defence development.

b. Proportional Allocation: The defence budget must be balanced, considering various defence programmes' priorities and requirements. It should reflect the needs for research and development (R&D), acquisition of new technologies, infrastructure investment, and capacity building. By ensuring proportional allocation, the defence budget can support a comprehensive approach to defence Emiratisation and address both short-term operational needs and long-term strategic goals.

c. Long-term Planning: Defence budget allocation should also prioritise long-term planning to ensure sustainability in defence Emiratisation efforts. This involves considering the lifecycle costs of defence programmes, including maintenance, upgrades, and replacements. By accounting for long-term planning, the defence budget can avoid short-sighted decision-making and enable the gradual development of self-reliance in defence capabilities.

d. Contingency Planning: Allocating resources for contingency planning is crucial to address unforeseen events or emergencies.

By setting aside a portion of the defence budget for contingency purposes, the UAE can respond effectively to crises, such as natural disasters or sudden security threats. Contingency planning ensures the availability of resources for rapid mobilisation and response, bolstering national security readiness.

3. Research and Development:

a. Investment in Innovation: A significant portion of resources needs to be allocated to research and development (R&D) activities. This enables the development of cutting-edge technologies and local defence equipment. R&D facilitates long-term sustainability and reduces reliance on foreign suppliers. Allocating resources for innovative projects, technology incubators, and partnerships with academic institutions can drive breakthroughs in defence technology and maintain a competitive edge.

b. Collaboration and Partnerships: Allocating resources for collaboration with international partners, research institutions, and academia can enhance innovation and knowledge transfer, enabling the UAE to accelerate its defence Emiratisation efforts. Joint research and development programmes, technology exchange initiatives, and partnerships with defence industries in friendly nations can leverage expertise and resources, reducing duplication of efforts and fostering a collaborative ecosystem.

c. Intellectual Property Rights: Allocating resources to protect intellectual property rights is essential to safeguard the investments in defence technology development. This involves implementing robust legal frameworks, establishing patents and trademarks, and creating mechanisms for technology transfer agreements. By protecting intellectual property, the UAE can attract foreign investments, encourage technology transfers, and foster a supportive domestic defence technology development ecosystem.

4. *Industrial Infrastructure:*

a. Establishing Defence Industrial Complexes: Allocating resources for establishing and maintaining defence industrial complexes is crucial for achieving self-reliance in defence production. This includes building manufacturing facilities, testing laboratories, and other necessary infrastructure to support local defence manufacturing capabilities. By investing in industrial parks and cluster development, the UAE can create a conducive environment for defence manufacturing, attract foreign direct investment, and encourage the growth of a robust defence industry ecosystem.

b. Skilling and Training Programmes: Resources must be allocated for skilling and training programmes to develop a skilled workforce capable of utilising the advanced technologies and techniques required in the defence industry. This includes investing in vocational training institutes, specialised defence education centres, and skill development programmes that align with the evolving needs of the defence sector. Collaborations with international training institutes and knowledge transfer initiatives can further enhance the quality and relevance of defence-related education and training.

c. Cybersecurity Infrastructure: Allocating resources for developing robust cybersecurity infrastructure is critical in defending against cyber threats, which have become increasingly prevalent in the digital age. Investment in advanced cyber defence technologies, establishing cybersecurity centres, and recruiting skilled personnel can strengthen the resilience of the defence industry against cyberattacks. By integrating cybersecurity measures into the industrial infrastructure, the UAE can protect sensitive defence information and maintain the integrity of its defence capabilities.

5. *Acquisition and Procurement:*

a. Balancing Imports and Local Production: The allocation of resources for defence procurement must balance imports and local production. It involves assessing the capabilities and capacity of the domestic defence industry and making informed decisions on what to source domestically and what can be procured from abroad. By prioritising the development of local capabilities and utilising international partnerships for technology transfers, the UAE can reduce reliance on foreign suppliers while ensuring access to critical technologies, leading to greater self-sufficiency in defence production.

b. Quality Control and Assurance: Allocating resources for quality control and assurance is vital to ensure that local defence equipment meets international standards and requirements. Implementing robust quality management systems, investing in certification processes, and establishing accreditation bodies can ensure the reliability and safety of defence products. Additionally, allocating resources for independent testing and evaluation centres can enhance the credibility and competitiveness of local defence equipment, facilitating their export potential.

c. Offset Programmes: Allocating resources for offset programmes can effectively leverage defence procurements for technology transfer and industrial development. Offsets require foreign defence suppliers to fulfil specified commitments to the local economy, such as investments in local manufacturing, technology transfers, or job creation. By strategically designing and implementing offset programmes, the UAE can benefit from defence procurements and enhance its local capabilities.

6. *Monitoring and Evaluation:*

a. Performance Monitoring: Allocating resources for monitoring and evaluation allows for assessing the effectiveness and efficiency of defence Emiratisation efforts. Regular performance monitoring helps identify areas of improvement and make necessary adjustments to resource allocation.

Through data-driven analysis, key performance indicators, and benchmarking exercises, policymakers can evaluate the outcomes of resource allocation decisions, identify bottlenecks, and optimise future resource allocation strategies.

b. Lessons Learnt and Feedback Loop: Allocating resources for feedback mechanisms and lessons learnt exercises promotes continuous improvement and enhances the effectiveness of resource allocation. Regular assessments, stakeholder consultations, and post-project evaluations enable informed decision-making and facilitate knowledge sharing across different defence programmes. Establishing a feedback loop ensures that successes are replicated, challenges are addressed, and resource allocation strategies are continuously refined, paving the way for sustainable and efficient defence Emiratisation.

In conclusion, allocating resources in the defence industry is a complex and dynamic process. It requires careful consideration of strategic priorities, defence budget allocation, research and development, industrial infrastructure, acquisition and procurement, and monitoring and evaluation. By aligning resource allocation with national security objectives, considering long-term planning, fostering innovation, investing in industrial infrastructure and skills development, balancing imports and local production, and implementing effective monitoring and evaluation mechanisms, the UAE can successfully develop its local defence capabilities and achieve self-reliance in the defence sector.

Efficient resource allocation is crucial in achieving defence Emiratisation and strengthening national security. By strategically prioritising defence programmes and assessing potential threats, the UAE can allocate resources towards the areas that require immediate attention and long-term development. This involves analysing geopolitical dynamics, assessing military capabilities, and evaluating emerging technologies to ensure resource allocation aligns with the evolving security landscape.

The defence budget serves as the primary funding source for defence Emiratisation efforts. Therefore, it is essential to identify the different funding sources and allocate resources balanced. Proportional allocation of the defence budget ensures that resources are allocated to research and development, acquisition of new technologies, infrastructure investment, and capacity building. The UAE can enhance its defence capabilities by considering long-term planning, allocating resources for contingency purposes, and effectively responding to unforeseen events.

Investment in research and development is essential for developing local defence capabilities. Allocating resources for innovative projects, collaborating with international partners, and protecting intellectual property rights enable the UAE to develop cutting-edge technologies and reduce reliance on foreign suppliers. Furthermore, allocating resources for establishing defence industrial complexes, skilling and training programmes, and cybersecurity infrastructure strengthens the industrial base and ensures the availability of a skilled workforce capable of utilising advanced technologies. The allocation of resources for defence acquisition and procurement requires striking a balance between imports and local production. By prioritising the development of local capabilities and utilising international partnerships for technology transfers, the UAE can reduce reliance on foreign suppliers while ensuring access to critical technologies. Quality control and assurance and the implementation of offset programmes further enhance the credibility and competitiveness of local defence equipment.

Monitoring and evaluation play a crucial role in resource allocation. Allocating resources for performance monitoring allows policymakers to assess the effectiveness and efficiency of defence Emiratisation efforts. By learning from experiences and creating a feedback loop, the UAE can continuously improve resource allocation strategies and ensure their sustainability and effectiveness.

In summary, allocating resources in the defence industry is a multifaceted process that requires careful consideration of strategic priorities, the defence budget, research and development, industrial infrastructure, acquisition and procurement, and monitoring and evaluation. By effectively allocating resources, the UAE can strengthen its defence capabilities, reduce reliance on foreign suppliers, and achieve self-reliance in the defence sector, ultimately enhancing national security and sovereignty.

IX

Implications for the National Economy

A. ECONOMIC DIVERSIFICATION THROUGH DEFENSE EMIRATISATION

Establishing and growing a thriving defence industry in the UAE has far-reaching implications for the national economy. Historically dependent on sectors such as oil and tourism, defence Emiratisation provides a unique opportunity to diversify the economy and reduce its reliance on finite resources. By creating a robust defence industry, the UAE can tap into new areas of economic growth, generate employment opportunities, and attract foreign direct investment.

1. Stimulating Economic Growth: Developing local defence capabilities requires significant research and development (R&D) investment, infrastructure, and human capital. This, in turn, stimulates domestic economic activity as government and private sector investments flow into these areas. Through R&D, local defence companies actively engage in scientific discovery, technological advancements, and product

innovation. These efforts have a spillover effect that can benefit other industries, facilitating the development of high-tech manufacturing capabilities, fostering innovation, and driving overall economic growth.

The UAE government's commitment to defence Emiratisation is evident through its significant investments in R&D institutions, defence manufacturing facilities, and infrastructure development. Institutions like the UAE's Artificial Intelligence Research Centre and the Dubai Future Foundation's Accelerators programme provide a platform for harnessing cutting-edge technologies and attracting talent. Such initiatives strengthen the foundations for a knowledge-based economy and position the UAE as a hub for research and innovation.

Moreover, the growth of the defence industry attracts foreign investment and encourages partnerships with international defence companies. This collaboration brings expertise, technology transfers, and access to global markets. As international defence players establish a presence in the UAE, they contribute through direct investment and creating avenues for joint ventures and knowledge-sharing. These partnerships enhance the UAE's competitive advantage, accelerating economic growth and paving the way for future diversification.

2. Fostering a Knowledge-based Economy: The growth of the defence industry encourages the formation of a knowledge-based economy. It necessitates a highly skilled workforce with expertise in specialised fields such as engineering, manufacturing, cybersecurity, artificial intelligence, and data analytics. As local defence companies innovate and expand, they contribute to developing these critical skills and expertise, creating a pool of talent capable of driving innovation and competitiveness across multiple sectors of the economy. This enhances the UAE's technological capabilities and attracts global talent and foreign investment, further diversifying and strengthening the knowledge-based economy.

The UAE recognises the importance of investing in human capital to cultivate a knowledge-based economy. To this end, the government has implemented various initiatives to develop a skilled workforce. The National Defence Education and Training Council coordinates efforts to provide educational programmes and career pathways, aligning them with the needs of the defence industry. Vocational training centres, technical schools, and universities offer specialised programmes to equip individuals with the necessary skills for defence-related occupations. Additionally, partnerships with local and international educational institutions ensure that the workforce receives training in the latest technologies, promoting a seamless knowledge transfer to industry.

B. JOB CREATION AND SKILL DEVELOPMENT

Defence Emiratisation directly and positively impacts employment opportunities within the UAE. The development and expansion of the defence industry create a demand for a highly skilled workforce, ranging from engineers and researchers to technicians and manufacturing workers. As the defence sector increases its contribution to the national economy, it reduces unemployment rates. It fosters the creation of quality jobs across various skill levels and sectors. This helps to build a more resilient and inclusive economy by reducing dependency on foreign labour and enhancing the country's human capital.

1. Knowledge Transfer and Skill Development: The growth of the defence industry often involves partnerships between international defence companies and local entities. These collaborations facilitate the transfer of knowledge, expertise, and best practices to the UAE. Local professionals can work side-by-side with global experts, learning from their experience and gaining exposure to cutting-edge technologies and methodologies. The knowledge and skills acquired during these partnerships are valuable, as they can be applied within the defence

sector and throughout the broader economy, driving innovation and competitiveness.

To ensure continuous skill development, the UAE government has established centres of excellence in collaboration with leading international defence companies and research institutions. These centres serve as platforms for knowledge exchange and skills enhancement, offering training programmes, workshops, and joint research projects. As professionals engage in these initiatives, they acquire specialised skills, expand their expertise, and contribute to the overall growth of the defence ecosystem.

2. Sustainable Skill Development: Developing local defence capabilities necessitates a sustained investment in skill development programmes. These initiatives encompass vocational training, apprenticeships, internships, and educational programmes tailored to the specific needs of the defence industry. The UAE ensures a continuous supply of skilled labour by equipping individuals with the necessary skills and competencies. Additionally, the emergence of a thriving defence industry creates a "pull effect" by attracting talented domestic and international individuals who are interested in pursuing careers within the sector. This enhances the UAE's human capital and contributes to its long-term economic development.

Recognising the importance of ongoing skill development, the UAE government has implemented comprehensive programmes to bridge skill gaps and promote lifelong learning. The Abu Dhabi Polytechnic, for example, offers a range of technical and vocational courses in collaboration with the defence industry. These programmes provide students with the necessary skills for employment in the sector and support industry-specific skills upgrades for professionals already in the workforce. Such initiatives ensure that the UAE's defence industry has access to a highly skilled and adaptable labour force capable of meeting evolving demands and driving sustainable economic growth.

C. BROADER ECONOMIC IMPACTS

The establishment of a self-sufficient defence industry in the UAE has the potential to generate widespread economic benefits beyond direct defence-related activities.

1. Stimulating Local Businesses: As the defence industry grows, it creates opportunities for small and medium-sized enterprises (SMEs) to participate in the supply chain. These SMEs can provide various products and services, from components and materials to maintenance and logistical support. The involvement of local businesses in the defence supply chain generates additional revenue streams. It fosters entrepreneurship, innovation, and job creation. Moreover, the spill-over effects contribute to the growth and diversification of related industries, creating an ecosystem of interrelated economic activities.

To facilitate the participation of local businesses, the UAE government has implemented initiatives that promote SME growth and development. These include providing access to finance, fostering innovation, simplifying regulatory frameworks, and encouraging collaboration between SMEs and large corporations. The presence of a robust defence industry provides a reliable customer base for these SMEs, offering stability and opportunities for long-term business partnerships.

2. Technological Advancements and Innovation: Defence Emiratisation enhances the UAE's technological capabilities and fosters innovation. Local defence companies invest heavily in R&D to develop advanced technologies and maintain a competitive edge. These technological advancements have the potential to spill over into other sectors, such as aerospace, telecommunications, transportation, and advanced manufacturing. For instance, advances in materials science, robotics,

and AI-driven analytics within the defence sector can find applications in developing autonomous vehicles, smart cities, and sustainable energy systems. The resulting improvement in competitiveness strengthens the UAE's position as a regional leader in innovation and technology.

The UAE government collaborates closely with research institutions, defence companies, and academia to encourage technological advancements and innovation. Investment in research centres, incubators, and innovation hubs fosters an environment conducive to technological advances and creates opportunities for collaboration and knowledge-sharing. For example, the Dubai Future Accelerators programme connects government entities with innovative technology startups, allowing for developing and implementing cutting-edge solutions across various industries.

3. Export Potential: The growth of the defence industry in the UAE opens up opportunities for the export of local defence products and services. As local defence companies develop advanced technologies, they can compete in the global defence market and generate export revenue. This boosts the country's economic growth and enhances its international standing as a provider of high-quality defence solutions.

The UAE government actively supports the export potential of local defence companies through various policies and initiatives. This includes providing access to international markets, facilitating partnerships between local and international defence players, and promoting the export of locally developed defence technologies. With a focus on innovation and quality, the UAE's defence industry has the potential to establish a strong presence in the global defence market, further diversifying and strengthening the national economy.

D. Conclusion

Developing a self-sufficient defence industry in the UAE has significant implications for the national economy. It offers a unique opportunity for economic diversification, job creation, and skill development. The UAE government promotes economic growth and stimulates domestic financial activity by investing in research and development, infrastructure, and human capital. The growth of the defence industry also fosters a knowledge-based economy, attracting global talent and foreign investment and positioning the UAE as a hub for research, innovation, and technology.

Moreover, defence Emiratisation has broader economic impacts, including stimulating local businesses, technological advancements, and export potential. The involvement of local SMEs in the defence supply chain generates additional revenue streams, fosters entrepreneurship, and creates an ecosystem of interrelated economic activities. Technological advancements within the defence sector spill over into other industries, enhancing competitiveness and innovation. Finally, the growth of the defence industry opens up export opportunities, further boosting economic growth and establishing the UAE as a provider of high-quality defence solutions in the global market.

Developing a thriving defence industry in the UAE strengthens its security and defence capabilities and contributes to its long-term economic growth and sustainability. The UAE has recognised the importance of defence Emiratisation and continues to invest in initiatives that promote economic diversification, job creation, and skill development in this sector.

A. Economic Diversification through Defence Emiratisation

The United Arab Emirates' pursuit of defence Emiratisation holds significant implications for the country's economic diversification efforts. Historically dependent on oil exports, the UAE has recognised the importance of reducing its reliance on a single industry and diversifying its economy to ensure long-term sustainability and stability. Defence Emiratisation presents an opportunity to achieve this goal by creating new economic growth and development avenues.

One of the critical aspects of defence Emiratisation is the development of a domestic defence industry. The UAE aims to establish manufacturing facilities, research and development centres, and training institutes to support the production of defence equipment and technologies. This strategic move strengthens the country's defence capabilities and generates numerous socio-economic benefits.

By nurturing a robust domestic defence industry, the UAE can create new job opportunities and build a highly skilled workforce, boosting employment rates and income nationwide. The defence industry provides a range of career options in areas such as engineering, research and development, manufacturing, and technology. These opportunities benefit Emirati citizens and attract skilled professionals worldwide, fostering a diverse and vibrant workforce. Besides, defence Emiratisation prompts the growth of local supply chains and various ancillary industries. Establishing a domestic defence industry requires raw materials, components, and subsystems to be sourced locally. This leads to developing and expanding local suppliers and vendors, stimulating economic activity in engineering, manufacturing, logistics, and specialised services. The growth of these ancillary industries generates employment and contributes to the overall diversification of the UAE's economy.

To support the growth of the domestic defence industry, the UAE has implemented various policies and initiatives to attract foreign direct investment (FDI) and encourage the establishment of joint ventures with international defence companies. The UAE can benefit from technology transfer, knowledge exchange, and access to global markets by actively engaging with global defence manufacturers. Foreign investment brings capital, expertise, and advanced technologies, further strengthening the UAE's defence industry and translating into spillover effects for the broader economy.

Foreign direct investment bolsters the UAE's positioning as a regional defence production and research hub. It promotes economic growth in the larger region. As international defence companies set up operations in the UAE, they create additional job opportunities and knowledge-sharing. The presence of these companies also enhances the country's reputation as a centre of excellence in defence manufacturing, attracting further investment and fostering a competitive ecosystem of innovation and research.

Moreover, defence Emiratisation emphasises innovation and technological advancements. Research and development (R&D) activities have become essential to developing a robust domestic defence industry.

The UAE has made significant investments in R&D by establishing dedicated centres of excellence and collaborating with renowned international institutions. These collaborative efforts facilitate the transfer of knowledge and expertise, promoting technological advancements and enhancing the country's defence capabilities. This focus on innovation enhances the country's defence capabilities and drives advancements in civilian applications. Breakthroughs in cybersecurity, artificial intelligence, and renewable energy, initially developed for defence purposes, can potentially revolutionise various other sectors. For example, developing cybersecurity technologies can strengthen digital infrastructure and safeguard critical sectors such as banking, telecommunications, and energy. Advances in renewable energy technologies initially explored for defence purposes, can now be applied to promote sustainable practices and reduce carbon emissions across the UAE and beyond. These cross-sectoral applications contribute to the overall economic diversification agenda and position the UAE as a leader in critical technological domains.

Furthermore, defence Emiratisation plays a crucial role in developing a knowledge-based economy. By investing in R&D, the UAE fosters a culture of innovation, entrepreneurship, and knowledge transfer. This creates a highly skilled workforce that can contribute to multiple sectors beyond defence. The expertise gained through defence Emiratisation can be leveraged to position the UAE as a regional centre of excellence in various high-tech industries such as information technology, advanced manufacturing, aerospace, and renewable energy. This expansion into non-defence sectors creates a multiplier effect, driving economic diversification and enhancing the resilience of the UAE's economy.

The economic impact of defence Emiratisation extends beyond the borders of the UAE. As the country establishes itself as a regional hub for defence production and innovation, it can attract international partners, investors, and customers. This bolsters the economy and strengthens the UAE's position as a prominent player in the global defence industry. The UAE can generate revenue and influence economic growth in the larger region by exporting defence products and technologies. Providing defence-related services, such as maintenance, repair, and overhaul, can also contribute significantly to the UAE's export earnings and create a globally competitive defence ecosystem.

However, it is essential to acknowledge the challenges associated with defence Emiratisation and economic diversification. Developing a robust defence industry requires significant investment, technology transfer, and expertise. The UAE must effectively navigate potential roadblocks such as budgetary constraints, regulatory frameworks, and competition from established global defence manufacturers.

To address these challenges, the UAE has implemented policies and initiatives that create an enabling environment for defence Emiratisation, including strategic partnerships, defence offsets, and industry-specific collaborations. Establishing strategic alliances with leading global defence companies allows the UAE to leverage their expertise and access cutting-edge technologies. Defence offsets, where international companies are required to invest a portion of the contract value back into the UAE's economy, contribute to the growth of local industries and promote knowledge transfer.

Additionally, continuous investment in research and development, education, and skills training will ensure a steady talent supply and support technological advancement in the long run. The UAE's commitment to education and development is evident through initiatives such as establishing specialised defence academies, collaborations with international educational institutions, and investment in vocational training programmes.

These efforts ensure a pipeline of skilled professionals who can contribute to the growth and sustainability of the defence industry and other sectors, driving economic diversification.

In conclusion, defence Emiratisation serves as a catalyst for economic diversification in the UAE. Establishing a domestic defence industry, coupled with innovation, technology transfer, and foreign investment, creates a ripple effect across various sectors, strengthening the economy and reducing reliance on oil revenues. By leveraging defence-industry capabilities, the UAE can build a resilient and sustainable economy that thrives on knowledge, innovation, and global competitiveness. Effective defence Emiratisation strategies and policies will contribute to long-term economic growth, securing a prosperous future for the UAE and its people.

B. Job Creation and Skill Development

Defence Emiratisation in the UAE is a multifaceted process that enhances national security and stimulates job creation, economic growth, and technological advancements. As the country continues to strengthen its defence capabilities and reduce reliance on imports, the job market and workforce are undergoing significant transformations to meet the demands of a growing defence industry.

Job creation in the defence sector goes beyond traditional roles such as soldiers and officers. The establishment and expansion of defence-related industries, including manufacturing, research and development, technology, and cybersecurity, have resulted in various employment opportunities for professionals across multiple fields. Engineers specialising in aerospace, electrical, and mechanical disciplines can find work in developing and maintaining sophisticated defence systems. In contrast, material and chemical engineers contribute to producing advanced materials used in defence technologies. Scientists and researchers support defence innovation, leveraging their weapon systems, artificial intelligence, and nanotechnology expertise to advance the country's defence capabilities.

Moreover, the defence industry's expansion also influences job creation in ancillary sectors. Logistics, supply chain management, transportation, and construction industries experience increased demand as they support the infrastructure and operations necessary for defence manufacturing and deployment. Maintenance and repair services for defence equipment generate opportunities for skilled technicians to ensure technologies' longevity and optimal functioning. This ripple effect extends to various professions, including IT specialists, project managers, legal advisors, and financial experts, who play critical roles in supporting the defence industry's growth.

To meet the evolving demands of the defence industry, skill development is prioritised through comprehensive training and education initiatives. Collaborations between defence organisations, universities, and vocational institutions allow designing and implementing tailored programmes that address the sector's specific needs. These programmes provide hands-on training, laboratory facilities, and access to state-of-the-art technologies to equip individuals with the skills and knowledge required for defence-oriented careers. Internships and apprenticeships further bridge the gap between classroom learning and practical experience, allowing aspiring professionals to gain valuable insights and build industry connections.

The UAE's commitment to defence Emiratisation also fosters technological advancements and innovation. By promoting a culture of research and development, the country prioritises creating and adopting cutting-edge technologies that enhance national security and propel economic growth. Research institutions and defence organisations collaborate closely, sharing knowledge and expertise to drive breakthroughs in unmanned systems, cybersecurity, space exploration, and renewable energy. In partnership with academic institutions, the government actively promotes STEM (Science, Technology, Engineering, and Mathematics) education to cultivate the next generation of innovators and entrepreneurs. Specialised centres of excellence and research programmes are established to accelerate technological advancements further within the defence sector.

While defence Emiratisation brings numerous benefits, it also challenges ensuring the alignment between workforce skills and industry needs. Technological advancements necessitate continuous upskilling and reskilling programmes to ensure professionals stay abreast of the latest developments. The government and private sector must collaborate to develop a responsive and adaptable educational ecosystem to anticipate and address skill gaps effectively. Diverse training opportunities, such as online courses, boot camps, and certification programmes, are essential to cater to individuals seeking flexible learning pathways.

In promoting job creation and skill development, the UAE recognises the importance of diversity and inclusivity within the defence industry. Efforts are made to address gender disparities and encourage the participation and representation of women in defence-related professions. Women's empowerment programmes, mentorship initiatives, and scholarships are designed to provide equal opportunities for women to contribute to and excel in the defence industry. The UAE harnesses various perspectives and talents by fostering a diverse and inclusive workforce, enhancing innovation and problem-solving capabilities.

In conclusion, defence Emiratisation in the UAE has far-reaching implications in bolstering national security and job creation, economic growth, and technological advancements. The development of the defence sector results in a broad spectrum of employment opportunities, ranging from highly specialised fields to ancillary industries. Through strategic collaborations and focused educational programmes, the UAE is building a skilled and adaptable workforce capable of driving innovation in the defence industry, contributing to overall economic growth, and fostering technological advancements. By promoting diversity and equal opportunity, the UAE ensures that the benefits of defence Emiratisation are accessible to all, ultimately contributing to a thriving and inclusive society.

C. Broader Economic Impacts

The Emiratisation of the defence industry in the UAE has far-reaching and profound economic implications that extend beyond national security. This chapter delves deeper into the broader economic impacts of defence Emiratisation, examining how it contributes to the national economy's growth, diversification, and sustainability.

One of the primary economic benefits of defence Emiratisation is the creation of job opportunities and the development of a highly skilled workforce. As the UAE invests in developing its domestic defence capabilities, it opens employment opportunities across various sectors. Establishing local defence manufacturing facilities creates jobs for engineers, technicians, and skilled labourers. It provides stability and long-term career prospects to individuals. By offering stable incomes, these employment opportunities improve the overall standard of living for the workforce, consequently boosting consumption and driving demand within the economy. Furthermore, developing local defence technologies requires a highly skilled workforce, leading to the growth of educational institutions, training programmes, and vocational centres that focus on advanced technical skills. This deliberate investment in human capital enhances the country's overall competitiveness and positions it as a hub for innovation and cutting-edge technology development.

Defence Emiratisation also plays a pivotal role in driving economic diversification by reducing the country's reliance on a single sector, such as oil and gas. By investing in developing local defence capabilities, the UAE expands its economic base and establishes an alternative source of revenue. The defence industry catalyses the growth of related sectors, such as research and development, technology, manufacturing, and logistics. This generates a multiplier effect within the economy, attracting investment, fostering innovation, and promoting productivity. The growth and diversification of these industries contribute to transforming the UAE into a knowledge-based economy capable of adapting to global economic changes and fluctuations. By reducing dependence on oil and gas revenue, defence Emiratisation mitigates the risks associated with an over-reliance on a single industry, making the economy more resilient and sustainable in the long run.

Furthermore, defence Emiratisation promotes establishing and growing technology clusters and innovation ecosystems in the UAE. The process of developing local defence capabilities necessitates technological advancements, which in turn drive research and development activities. These activities address the defence industry's specific needs and spillover effects on other sectors. For example, advancements in aerospace manufacturing techniques developed for defence can be applied to the broader aviation industry, enabling the UAE to become a regional hub for aerospace manufacturing and maintenance. Similarly, innovations in cybersecurity and data analytics developed for defence applications find applications in various sectors, including finance, healthcare, transportation, and smart cities. This technology transfer from the defence industry to other sectors stimulates innovation, enhances productivity, improves overall competitiveness, and attracts foreign direct investment, enriching the UAE's economic landscape.

The Emiratisation of the defence industry also fosters the growth of small and medium-sized enterprises (SMEs) within the country.

Collaborations between giant defence corporations and smaller, specialised firms in developing local defence supply chains provide opportunities for SMEs to participate and excel in the defence sector. These collaborations not only create new markets and export opportunities but also stimulate entrepreneurship and promote the growth of the private sector. The influx of innovative ideas and technologies from these SMEs strengthens the overall resilience of the economy. It enhances its capacity to weather economic downturns. Moreover, defence Emiratisation encourages the localisation of supply chains, reducing import dependence and fostering a wide range of domestic industries catering to the needs of the defence sector. This localisation further strengthens the country's economic sovereignty and resilience.

In addition to the direct economic benefits, defence Emiratisation significantly impacts the national trade balance. As the UAE develops its domestic defence capabilities, it reduces its reliance on imported equipment and systems. This shift towards local production and procurement saves foreign exchange reserves and generates export opportunities. Developing local defence technologies opens doors for exports to other nations seeking advanced defence solutions. This enhances the country's exports and bolsters its reputation as a reliable supplier of cutting-edge defence technologies, resulting in positive trade balances and further strengthening its international standing as a trusted defence industry player.

Moreover, defence Emiratisation significantly contributes to the growth of the UAE's research and development (R&D) sector. As the country invests in developing local defence capabilities, it spawns a conducive environment for R&D activities and technological advancements. This leads to establishing research centres, institutes, and partnerships focusing on defence technology and innovation. The R&D sector benefits from increased funding, collaboration with industry experts, and access to cutting-edge equipment and facilities.

This attracts skilled researchers, encourages knowledge creation, and strengthens the UAE's position as a hub for innovation in the defence and technology sectors. The growth of the R&D sector in defence Emiratisation efforts spills over into other sectors, fostering a culture of innovation and providing a competitive edge to the UAE in various global industries.

In conclusion, defence Emiratisation in the UAE has profound and multi-faceted impacts on the broader economy. It creates job opportunities, develops a highly skilled workforce, drives economic diversification, and stimulates the growth of SMEs. Furthermore, it promotes innovation and technological advancements, improves trade balance, and significantly contributes to expanding the research and development sector. These economic benefits strengthen the UAE's economy's overall growth, resilience, and sustainability, positioning it as a global player in the defence industry and fostering prosperity for its citizens. As the UAE continues its Emiratisation efforts, it must capitalise on these economic impacts, leverage them strategically, and forge partnerships to propel sustained economic growth and development for the benefit of future generations.

X

Geopolitical Ramifications for the Gulf Region

The defence Emiratisation efforts in the UAE have significant geopolitical implications for the Gulf region. As the UAE seeks to build its local defence capabilities, it will inevitably impact the area's power dynamics, regional alliances, and international relations.

One of the immediate effects of defence Emiratisation is the potential recalibration of alliances. The Gulf region has long relied on external powers for security support, with the United States playing a prominent role. However, the UAE's pursuit of defence self-sufficiency challenges this traditional reliance. It signals a desire for greater autonomy in its security affairs. This shift in alliances may lead to reevaluating existing relationships and realigning regional power dynamics as countries reassess their strategic partnerships.

Furthermore, the UAE's ambition to become a significant player in the defence industry can potentially disrupt the traditional balance of power in the Gulf. As it strengthens its military capabilities through

Emiratisation, the UAE emerges as a critical actor in the region, capable of exerting more influence and actively shaping security dynamics. This newfound influence can contribute to stability and deterrence as the UAE becomes more confident in protecting its interests. However, it also raises concerns among neighbouring states, who may perceive this as challenging their power and influence, leading to potential tensions and rivalries.

Moreover, defence Emiratisation in the UAE can have broader implications for international relations. Historically, arms imports have been a significant part of the Gulf nations' defence strategies, with major defence manufacturers, such as the United States, playing a dominant role in supplying the region. However, the UAE's shift towards self-reliance disrupts this dynamic, potentially leading to increased competition in the global defence market. As the UAE develops its defence industry, it may seek partnerships and collaborations with other countries, signalling a new era of diversification in the Gulf arms market. This shift could create opportunities and challenges as traditional suppliers face new competition and alternative sources of defence equipment emerge.

Furthermore, the success of the UAE in defence of Emiratisation could inspire other Gulf states to follow suit. As the UAE progresses towards defence self-sufficiency, it sets an example for other countries seeking to enhance their security autonomy. This could create a more multipolar defence landscape in the Gulf, with each country striving for self-sufficiency and reduced reliance on external powers. Such a shift could impact alliances and partnerships as Gulf nations forge new relationships based on shared technological advancements and defence ambitions. This may lead to increased regional assertiveness and competition as countries vie for influence and seek to position themselves as significant players in the defence industry.

In summary, the defence Emiratisation efforts in the UAE have profound and far-reaching geopolitical ramifications for the Gulf region. They challenge the existing power dynamics, incentivise a potential realignment of alliances, impact international relations, and may inspire other Gulf states to pursue similar paths. As the UAE propels itself forward in its journey towards defence self-sufficiency, the geopolitical landscape of the Gulf region will undoubtedly be reshaped, with implications for both the regional and international security architecture.

A. Recalibration of Alliances in Defence Emiratisation

The process of defence Emiratisation in the United Arab Emirates (UAE) has instigated a significant recalibration of alliances in the defence sector as the country strives to reduce its dependence on foreign suppliers and enhance its strategic autonomy. This recalibration involves forging new relationships and strengthening existing ones based on mutual interests, technological ambitions, and the evolving dynamics of the global defence industry, ultimately shaping a new landscape of defence partnerships.

One noteworthy aspect of this recalibration is the UAE's increasing engagement with emerging defence industries in India, South Korea, and Turkey. These nations have demonstrated commendable expertise in developing local defence capabilities and possess advanced technologies that align with the UAE's ambitions. Through joint ventures, technology transfers, and collaborative research and development projects, the UAE has effectively tapped into the knowledge and capabilities of these countries, leveraging their expertise to bolster its defence capabilities.

In India, the UAE has established partnerships with leading defence manufacturers and research institutions, collaborating on projects ranging from armoured vehicles to aerospace technologies. This mutually beneficial relationship allows the UAE to access India's advanced research and manufacturing facilities. At the same time, India benefits from the UAE's expertise in areas such as unmanned systems and cybersecurity. The partnership also extends to joint military exercises and training programmes, fostering closer ties and interoperability between the armed forces of both nations.

Similarly, the UAE has found a valuable defence partner in South Korea, a global leader in aerospace, naval systems, and advanced electronics. Through joint ventures and technology transfers, the UAE has gained access to South Korea's cutting-edge defence technologies, enhancing its missile systems, naval vessels, and cyber defence capabilities. Both nations have recognised the synergy between their defence industries. They actively explore avenues for increased collaboration, including joint research and development initiatives.

Turkey has become a key partner for the UAE with its growing defence industry and expertise in manufacturing diverse defence platforms. The two countries have formed alliances in various domains, including the development of armoured vehicles, drones, and advanced munitions. Notably, the UAE has extended its collaboration with Turkey by leveraging Turkey's strong foothold in the defence sector to expand its market reach and export capabilities, bolstering its domestic defence industry and contributing to its economic growth.

While engaging with emerging defence industries, the UAE is equally committed to maintaining its longstanding partnerships with traditional defence suppliers, including the United States, the United Kingdom, and France. These alliances have provided advanced defence technologies, equipment, and knowledge transfer to the UAE's armed forces.

Recognising the UAE's growing focus on defence Emiratisation and strategic autonomy, these partners have embraced a collaborative approach, emphasising technology sharing and fostering a more balanced and mutually beneficial alliance. For instance, the UAE and the United States have partnered on missile defence systems, cybersecurity, and advanced avionics projects, giving the UAE greater control over its defence capabilities while leveraging American expertise.

Moreover, the UAE has been actively diversifying its defence partnerships by engaging with non-traditional players in the global defence industry. This includes countries like China and Russia, which have made remarkable strides in developing advanced defence technologies. Through joint exercises, military exchanges, bilateral agreements, and technology transfers, the UAE aims to tap into a broader range of defence capabilities, ensure access to alternative suppliers, and reduce vulnerabilities associated with overreliance on a single source. By exploring partnerships with these nations, the UAE becomes a catalyst for diversifying the global defence industry, contributing to a more multipolar and inclusive paradigm. These new partnerships strengthen the UAE's position in global defence discussions and provide joint research and development opportunities, benefiting the UAE and its new partners.

However, navigating the intricacies of this recalibration process is not without its challenges. Traditional defence partners may harbour concerns about the UAE's increasing focus on defence Emiratisation, fearing a potential impact on their arms sales and regional influence. Geopolitical dynamics also come into play, as the UAE's choices of defence partners may be seen aligning with certain regional powers, potentially causing tensions with others.

Thus, the UAE must tread carefully, balancing its ambitions for defence Emiratisation with maintaining stable and constructive relationships with its allies.

Nonetheless, the recalibration of alliances presents an opportunity for greater cooperation and innovation in the defence sector. By sharing expertise, technologies, and resources with its partners, the UAE can collectively keep pace with global advancements, contribute to regional stability, and address shared security challenges. This recalibration allows for increased interoperability, joint military exercises, and training programmes, fostering closer ties and trust between nations. It also serves as a platform for collaborative research and development initiatives, leading to breakthrough innovations and advancements that benefit all parties involved.

Ultimately, the process of defence Emiratisation in the UAE necessitates a comprehensive recalibration of alliances in the defence sector. By diversifying partnerships, engaging with emerging defence industries, and maintaining robust relationships with traditional suppliers, the UAE aims to enhance its technological capabilities, reduce dependencies, and ensure national security in an increasingly complex geopolitical landscape. This recalibration signifies the UAE's determination to become a leader in defence innovation, contributing to global advancements while safeguarding its interests. By strategically navigating this path, the UAE is poised to shape the future of the defence industry, strengthen international cooperation, and secure its position at the forefront of technological advancements in defence.

B. Power Dynamics in the Gulf

The power dynamics in the Gulf region have undergone significant shifts in recent years, influenced in part by the United Arab Emirates (UAE) commitment to defence Emiratisation. As the UAE strengthens its national defence capabilities and reduces its reliance on foreign suppliers, it impacts the balance of power within the Gulf region and on the broader international stage.

Historically, the Gulf has been a region where external actors, pre-eminent global powers, heavily influence power dynamics. Like other Gulf states, the UAE relied on foreign military assistance and imports to address security concerns. This dependence made the UAE vulnerable and susceptible to its foreign allies' changing priorities and policies.

However, with the introduction of defence Emiratisation measures, the UAE is asserting its autonomy and reducing its dependence on external powers. This shift in power dynamics has several implications that extend beyond just military capabilities.

Firstly, defence Emiratisation allows the UAE to have greater control over its defence strategies and decision-making processes.

The UAE can align its defence priorities with national security interests by developing local defence capabilities. This includes the ability to tailor defence procurement to specific operational requirements and investment in research and development to cultivate cutting-edge technologies. As the UAE leverages its homegrown talents, resources, and geographical advantages, it becomes more self-reliant and responsive to evolving security challenges.

The UAE has made significant progress in critical areas of defence Emiratisation, such as aerospace, maritime, and cybersecurity. In the aerospace sector, the UAE launched its own satellite and space agency, the UAE Space Agency, in 2014. The nation's first locally-produced military unmanned aircraft system, the "Yabhon," has also demonstrated the UAE's commitment to acquiring advanced aerospace technologies. Additionally, the UAE has invested in developing a robust maritime defence industry, expanding its naval fleet and constructing state-of-the-art naval vessels. This includes the locally-developed Ghannatha-class corvette with cutting-edge anti-ship and anti-air capabilities. Furthermore, the UAE has focused on bolstering its cybersecurity capabilities to defend against cyber threats, creating specialised institutions and fostering partnerships with leading global cybersecurity firms.

Secondly, the UAE's enhanced defence capabilities contribute to a more balanced power structure within the Gulf region. As the UAE strengthens its military, it is better positioned to deter potential threats or aggression from neighbouring states. This, in turn, can contribute to regional stability and reduce the likelihood of conflict. The UAE's commitment to defence Emiratisation also serves as an example to other countries in the region, inspiring them to invest in their military capabilities and fostering a sense of collective security within the Gulf Cooperation Council (GCC).

Moreover, the UAE's increased military prowess adds a new dimension to the power dynamics in the Gulf and reshapes regional alliances.

Traditionally, the Gulf has seen a power balance between Saudi Arabia and Iran, with each country seeking to influence the region.

However, as the UAE enhances its defence capabilities, it emerges as a significant player in its own right, challenging the traditional power dynamics. This increases the complexity of regional interactions and calls for a reassessment of geopolitical dynamics in the Gulf.

The pursuit of defence Emiratisation also has implications for the UAE's relationships with its traditional allies and partners. Given its strengthened defence capabilities, the UAE may seek to recalibrate its alliances and partnerships to reflect its newfound autonomy. While the UAE maintains strong ties with key allies such as the United States and France, it also actively pursues partnerships with other countries that can provide advanced military technologies, training, and knowledge transfer. This diversification of partnerships strengthens the UAE's position in the international arena. It ensures broader access to cutting-edge defence technologies while reducing its vulnerability to the fluctuations of any foreign actor's policies.

Internationally, the UAE's progress in defence Emiratisation elevates its status as a global player. As the UAE demonstrates its ability to develop advanced defence technologies and capabilities, it enhances its reputation as a regional power with influence beyond the Gulf. This can result in new opportunities for collaborations and partnerships on the global stage, potentially leading to a more balanced power distribution in international relations.

Ultimately, the pursuit of defence Emiratisation by the UAE has the potential to significantly alter power dynamics in the Gulf region. The UAE asserts its autonomy by reducing its reliance on foreign suppliers and strengthening its defence capabilities. It contributes to a more balanced power structure within the region.

The evolving power dynamics also impact the UAE's relationships with its allies and partners and its international standing as a global player. The outcomes and implications of these power shifts will undoubtedly shape the future of the Gulf region and the wider international arena.

C. Influence on International Relations

Defence Emiratisation in the UAE has significant implications for international relations beyond what has been discussed. This extended version explores these implications in even greater depth.

1. Technological Advancement and Innovation: The UAE's pursuit of defence Emiratisation involves substantial investment in research and development, fostering technological advancements and innovation. Investing in cutting-edge technologies, the UAE enhances its defence capabilities while positioning itself as a regional technology hub. This attracts foreign partners seeking access to advanced defence technologies, leading to collaborations, joint research projects, and technological exchanges. These partnerships strengthen the UAE's defence sector, deepen its diplomatic ties, and contribute to regional and global technological progress.

2. Economic Diversification and Trade: Defence Emiratisation efforts also contribute to the UAE's broader goal of economic diversification. A robust defence industry creates opportunities for local and foreign businesses, leading to job creation and increasing exports of defence equipment. This opens avenues for trade partnerships, foreign

direct investment, and technology transfers. The growing defence sector can also incentivise the development of complementary industries such as aerospace, engineering, and manufacturing, driving economic growth and boosting the UAE's position as a global economic player.

3. Defence Diplomacy and Strategic Partnerships: As the UAE develops its defence capabilities, it strengthens its defence diplomacy and strategic partnerships with other nations. The UAE's defence industry can be vital in fostering military and security cooperation agreements, joint ventures, and collaborative defence projects. The UAE builds trust and collaboration with its partners by sharing expertise, joint training programmes, and military exercises, enhancing regional stability and security. Additionally, defence collaboration can result in broader strategic partnerships that extend beyond the defence sector, including diplomatic, cultural, economic, and technological aspects.

4. Human Capital Development and Knowledge Economy: Defence Emiratisation necessitates the development of a highly skilled workforce within the UAE. This focus on human capital development extends beyond the defence industry, creating a knowledge-based economy. Investing in education and training programmes enhances the skill sets of Emirati citizens, fostering talent in scientific research, engineering, technology, and innovation. This skilled workforce contributes to the defence sector. It drives advancements in other industries, attracting foreign investment and promoting economic diversification.

5. Soft Power Projection: The UAE's defence Emiratisation efforts contribute to its soft power projection on the international stage. By actively developing its defence capabilities, the UAE is a responsible global actor committed to regional stability and security. The country's contributions to peacekeeping missions, counter-terrorism efforts, and humanitarian assistance enhance its standing and influence among the international community. These contributions also engender trust and foster solid diplomatic relations, enabling the UAE to shape regional and global security agendas actively.

6. Research Collaboration and Innovation Ecosystem: Developing an indigenised defence industry fosters research collaboration and supports the creation of an innovation ecosystem. The UAE's investment in research and development facilities, academic institutions, and technology parks creates an environment conducive to cross-disciplinary collaborations. This collaboration brings together experts, scientists, and innovators from diverse fields, fuelling the creation of game-changing technologies not only for the defence sector but across various industries. The resulting advancements can be shared globally, promoting international research collaboration and strengthening the UAE's position in cutting-edge technology development.

In conclusion, defence Emiratisation in the UAE has profound implications for international relations, extending beyond defence capabilities. It drives technological advancement, contributes to economic diversification, strengthens defence diplomacy, builds human capital, projects soft power, and fosters research collaboration. The UAE's pursuit of defence industrialisation enhances its defence posture. It influences regional and global dynamics, positioning the country as a key player in international relations.

XI

Conclusion

This book delved into the dynamic journey of defence Emiratisation in the United Arab Emirates (UAE). It examined its multifaceted implications for national security, defence strategies, and the economy. By exploring the historical context and the factors driving the shift from reliance on foreign defence imports to a focus on developing local defence capabilities, we have gained insight into the rationale behind this strategic imperative.

Economic factors are one of the fundamental motivations behind defence Emiratisation in the UAE. Developing a strong defence industry is seen as a means to propel economic growth, create job opportunities, and diversify the country's economy, reducing its historical dependence on oil revenue. This strategic approach aligns with the broader national initiatives to achieve economic resilience and sustainability.

The economic benefits of defence Emiratisation extend beyond the direct impacts on the defence sector. A thriving defence industry provides opportunities for local suppliers, skilled labour, and ancillary industries, resulting in a multiplier effect on the economy. Moreover, by fostering research and development in defence technologies, the UAE can create a knowledge-intensive economy, attracting international investments and talent.

Pursuing technological ambitions is crucial in the UAE's defence Emiratisation efforts. The country aspires to be at the forefront of innovation and technological advancements in the defence sector. By nurturing local capabilities, the UAE aims to develop cutting-edge technologies and enhance its research and development capabilities, creating a foundation for breakthroughs that can shape the future of defence.

The technological advancements resulting from defence Emiratisation have far-reaching implications beyond the defence sector. As the UAE develops advanced defence technologies, these can be leveraged for civilian applications, such as aerospace, renewable energy, and transportation. The spillover effects of defence-industry-driven innovation can catalyse the growth of other high-tech sectors, enhancing overall national competitiveness and contributing to the UAE's aspirations of becoming a global hub for innovation.

Geopolitical considerations also drive the push for defence Emiratisation. By reducing dependencies on foreign suppliers, the UAE enhances its strategic autonomy. It diminishes the vulnerabilities caused by political shifts or regional conflicts. This pursuit of self-sufficiency gives the UAE greater control over its defence acquisitions, enabling the country to respond more effectively to its unique security challenges and contribute to regional stability.

The strategic autonomy achieved through defence Emiratisation can also increase diplomatic agility and flexibility. The UAE can align its defence policies with its broader political objectives by possessing local defence capabilities and forging its path in regional and international security initiatives. This ability to tailor defence strategies to national interests enhances the UAE's role as a reliable and influential actor in the global arena.

The impact of defence Emiratisation on national defence strategies is significant. Defence policies must be reconfigured as the UAE develops and integrates local technologies and capabilities to align with these evolving dynamics. The country's military doctrines will adapt to incorporate these new technologies, requiring a careful reassessment of defence priorities and strategies. Moreover, this shift in defence capabilities will affect regional military cooperation as the UAE's defence needs and abilities become more localised.

The evolution of defence strategies in response to defence Emiratisation also provides opportunities for enhanced military effectiveness. The alignment of defence policies with local capabilities enables the UAE's armed forces to maximise the utility of their resources, ensuring that defence investments are efficiently utilised. Furthermore, integrating advanced technologies and local capabilities enables a greater focus on adaptability, agility, and interoperability, enhancing the UAE's ability to respond to emerging security challenges.

The performance of the national armed forces will be significantly enhanced through defence Emiratisation. Developing and utilising their technologies and capabilities will make the UAE's armed forces more self-reliant, agile, and resilient. Local defence capabilities enable the armed forces to customise and tailor solutions to their specific requirements, increasing effectiveness and flexibility in addressing emerging security challenges. Additionally, defence Emiratisation promotes the nurturing of local talent while fostering collaborations with international defence industry leaders, leading to a skilled workforce and knowledge transfer.

National defence budgets will experience substantial impacts due to defence Emiratisation efforts. While there may be an initial increase in investments in research and development, the long-term benefits include reduced reliance on foreign sources and potential cost savings. However, a comprehensive cost-benefit analysis must be conducted to ensure the efficient allocation of resources that aligns with national objectives and economic considerations. This requires striking a delicate balance between the immediate procurement needs and the long-term investment in building a sustainable and technologically advanced defence industry.

The implications of defence Emiratisation extend beyond the defence sector and have broader economic impacts. By stimulating the growth of a robust defence industry, the UAE can create job opportunities, develop a high-skilled labour force, and foster innovation-driven entrepreneurship. By developing local defence capabilities, the UAE can reduce its dependence on oil revenue, enhance economic diversification, and increase resilience to economic fluctuations. The defence industry's multiplier effect and sustained investment in research and development can contribute to creating a knowledge-based economy.

In the broader geopolitical context of the Gulf region, defence Emiratisation can lead to recalibrations of alliances and partnerships. As the UAE expands its local capabilities, it may become an attractive collaborator for regional and international partners, fostering greater collaboration and knowledge sharing. This shift in the defence landscape may also influence power dynamics within the Gulf, potentially leading to realignments in alliances and impacting regional international relations.

In conclusion, defence Emiratisation is a multifaceted and strategic imperative for the UAE. It offers numerous benefits, from reducing reliance on foreign suppliers and enhancing national security to stimulating economic growth and fostering technological advancements. Investing in local defence capabilities strengthens the UAE's strategic autonomy, adapts to changing geopolitical dynamics, and contributes to regional stability. However, realising these benefits requires strategic planning, effective resource allocation, and careful management of the challenges inherent in defence Emiratisation. By addressing these critical factors, the UAE is poised to forge ahead as a leading player in the global defence industry, shaping its destiny and contributing to a more secure and prosperous future.

A. Summary of Findings

This final chapter provides an in-depth overview of the essential findings and conclusions from our exhaustive analysis of defence Emiratisation in the United Arab Emirates (UAE). Throughout the preceding chapters, we have delved into the rich historical context, multifaceted motivations, national security implications, impact on national defence strategies, the evolution of military doctrines, the performance of the national armed forces, allocation of national defence budgets, economic importance, and the geopolitical ramifications of defence Emiratisation.

The UAE's pursuit of defence Emiratisation is driven by many factors deeply rooted in economic, technological, and geopolitical ambitions. Economically, the goal is to reduce the country's dependency on foreign suppliers and to foster the growth of a sustainable and competitive defence industry. By promoting local employment opportunities, generating technological advancements within the nation, and encouraging technology transfer from international partners, the UAE aims to enhance its economic resilience and build a knowledge-based defence industry that can compete globally.

The UAE aspires to develop cutting-edge defence capabilities at the technological forefront, driven by a vision of becoming a leading innovator and technology exporter in the defence sector.

The country invests extensively in research and development, forging partnerships with international defence firms and establishing academic institutions dedicated to advanced technological research. By harnessing the potential of emerging technologies such as artificial intelligence, unmanned systems, and cyber defence, the UAE seeks to position itself as a critical player in the international defence market and contribute to shaping the future of defence technologies.

Geopolitically, defence Emiratisation is vital to the UAE's broader strategic ambitions. With a rapidly evolving regional and global landscape, the country aims to achieve strategic autonomy and reduce reliance on external actors for defence capabilities. An independent defence industry allows the UAE to maintain control over its national security decision-making processes, ensuring its policies align with its specific security objectives and are agile enough to adapt to changing regional dynamics. Furthermore, defence Emiratisation enables the UAE to assert itself as a regional power, influencing the power dynamics within the Gulf region and contributing to regional stability.

The Emiratisation process has had profound implications for the UAE's national security. By reducing reliance on foreign suppliers, the country has significantly enhanced its defence autonomy, reducing vulnerabilities and strengthening its ability to respond to evolving threats. The developments in local defence capabilities have led to the adaptation of military doctrines, which now integrate new technologies and align closely with the UAE's unique defence needs. By customising its defence strategies, the UAE has effectively enhanced its ability to address emerging threats and positioned itself as a reliable partner in regional and international security efforts.

Defence Emiratisation has positively impacted the performance of the national armed forces. The UAE has significantly enhanced its military effectiveness and contributed to regional stability by developing local defence capabilities.

The expansion of defence research and development programmes and efforts to cultivate a skilled workforce have allowed the UAE to utilise advanced defence technologies and leverage its local capabilities effectively. However, challenges remain, including continuous innovation and adaptation, investment in personnel training programmes to match the evolving technologies, and maintaining a competitive edge in an ever-evolving international defence market.

The national defence budgets have experienced a substantial shift as resources are allocated towards defence Emiratisation endeavours. While the initial investments may appear higher, defence Emiratisation presents significant economic benefits in the long term. By cultivating a domestic defence industry, the UAE has sparked economic diversification, stimulated job creation, and fostered skill development. Furthermore, the growth of the defence industry has a broader economic impact, contributing to the development of the national economy and positioning the UAE as a hub for defence manufacturing and technology.

Geopolitically, the pursuit of defence Emiratisation brings about several profound implications. As the UAE achieves greater self-reliance in defence matters, a recalibration of alliances and relationships with foreign partners may become necessary. By reducing dependency on external actors, the UAE becomes more autonomous in defence decision-making processes, allowing it to assert its unique interests and strengthen its position as a key regional player. The Gulf region's power dynamics may also be influenced, as the UAE establishes itself as a regional power with advanced defence capabilities, potentially impacting regional order and stability. Additionally, defence Emiratisation has broader implications for international relations, as the UAE's assertive stance in the defence industry elevates its standing and interactions within the global community, positioning it as a capable and influential player in the worldwide defence landscape.

In conclusion, defence Emiratisation in the UAE represents an extraordinary shift in the country's defence landscape. The nuanced findings presented throughout this book highlight the multifaceted motivations driving this pursuit, the profound implications for national security, the impact on defence strategies and military doctrines, the enhanced performance of the national armed forces, the reallocation of defence budgets, the economic ramifications and benefits, as well as the broader geopolitical implications. As the UAE continues on its path of defence Emiratisation, it must remain vigilant, adaptable to changing dynamics, and seize emerging opportunities in the global defence industry. These efforts will be vital in sustaining and expanding its achievements in this transformative endeavour, further solidifying its position as a formidable force in the defence sector.

B. Future Prospects and Recommendations

As the UAE progresses toward defence Emiratisation, it is crucial to delve deeper into the prospects and provide comprehensive recommendations for further development.

1. STRENGTHENING RESEARCH AND DEVELOPMENT:

1.1 Enhancing Partnerships: The UAE should foster strong partnerships with local universities, research institutions, and private companies. Collaborative research and development centres should be established to bring experts from various fields together. Joint projects with academia and industry will enable knowledge sharing, technology transfer, and expedited development of critical defence technologies.

1.2 Investing in Advanced Technologies: The UAE should prioritise investments in emerging and disruptive technologies to maintain its competitive edge. For example, artificial intelligence (AI) can revolutionise military operations, while autonomous systems can enhance logistics and surveillance capabilities. Cybersecurity technologies will protect critical infrastructure, and space technologies can aid satellite communication and intelligence gathering. By staying at the forefront of these advancements, the UAE can strengthen its defence capabilities and remain a leader in the field.

1.3 Promoting Innovation: Creating an environment that fosters innovation is essential for the UAE's defence industry. Incubators and accelerators should be established to support defence-focused start-ups and provide them with the necessary resources, mentorship, and guidance. Financial incentives, grants, and research funding can further encourage innovation. Additionally, organising competitions and challenges will spur creativity and allow for identifying novel solutions to defence challenges.

2. COLLABORATION AND COOPERATION:

2.1 Strategic Partnerships: The UAE should seek partnerships with leading international defence manufacturers and technology leaders. By forming joint ventures, strategic alliances, and technology transfer agreements, the UAE can gain access to critical defence technologies and knowledge. These partnerships facilitate the acquisition of advanced capabilities and promote mutual benefits, such as job creation, skill development, and knowledge exchange.

2.2 Regional Defence Cooperation: The UAE should explore opportunities for enhanced defence collaboration within the Gulf Cooperation Council (GCC) countries and other regional partners. By establishing joint defence exercises, information-sharing mechanisms, and training programmes, the UAE can strengthen regional security and promote interoperability among military forces. Joint procurement projects can also leverage collective purchasing power and lead to cost savings while deepening regional defence ties.

3. HUMAN RESOURCES DEVELOPMENT:

3.1 Talent Attraction: The UAE should actively attract top talent from across the globe to work in its defence industry.

Competitive salaries, attractive benefits packages, and opportunities for professional growth should be provided to entice highly skilled individuals. Building partnerships with leading international defence schools and institutes can help establish the UAE as a destination for talent and facilitate the exchange of knowledge and best practices.

3.2 Domestic Skill Development: The UAE should invest in programmes that focus on developing the skills of its citizens in defence-related fields. Specialised training programmes should be offered to enhance technical knowledge and expertise. Scholarships and internships can provide hands-on experience and help cultivate a pool of skilled professionals. Collaboration with local educational institutions will ensure curricula align with defence sector needs, creating a talent pipeline in critical areas.

4. EXPORTING CAPABILITIES:

4.1 Marketing and Promotion: The UAE should establish a dedicated brand for its defence products and technologies, supported by effective marketing and promotional campaigns. Participation in international defence exhibitions, trade shows, and symposiums will help showcase the UAE's defence capabilities. Leveraging digital platforms, targeted advertising, and engaging with potential customers directly can effectively communicate the value and quality of UAE defence products.

4.2 Establishing Strategic Alliances: The UAE should proactively identify potential export markets and establish strategic alliances with countries seeking advanced defence equipment and technologies to expand its global reach. Building relationships based on trust and credibility is crucial.

Offering competitive pricing, after-sales support, and tailored solutions based on customer requirements will solidify the UAE's reliable and preferred supplier position. Establishing joint ventures or local production facilities in targeted markets can further strengthen the UAE's presence.

5. DEFENCE INDUSTRIAL BASE EXPANSION:

5.1 Sector Diversification: The UAE should aim to diversify its defence industrial base beyond aerospace and land systems. Emphasis should be placed on emerging sectors such as cybersecurity, electronic warfare, robotics, and unmanned systems. Investments and partnerships in these areas will ensure a comprehensive and technologically advanced defence ecosystem. Diversification will also contribute to economic growth by tapping into niche markets and attracting foreign investment.

5.2 Small and Medium Enterprises (SMEs): Supporting the growth of SMEs in the defence industry will bring numerous benefits. The UAE should provide targeted support to SMEs, such as access to financing, business development assistance, and preferential procurement policies. Collaboration between SMEs and larger defence companies can foster innovation, provide greater flexibility, and contribute to job creation and economic diversification.

6. STRATEGIC PLANNING AND LONG-TERM VISION:

6.1 National Strategy: The UAE should develop a comprehensive national defence-emiratisation strategy with well-defined objectives, measurable milestones, and clear timelines. This strategy should encompass short-term and long-term goals, outlining priorities for research and development, partnerships, talent development, and market expansion.

Regular reviews and updates based on evolving priorities, market dynamics, and geopolitical realities are crucial for successful implementation.

6.2 Geopolitical Considerations: The UAE should continue monitoring geopolitical developments and assessing emerging threats to align its defence Emiratisation efforts accordingly. Understanding market trends, geopolitical risks, and regional security challenges will help prioritise focus areas, identify potential partners, and make informed strategic decisions. Adapting flexibly to changing circumstances will ensure the UAE's defence industry remains resilient and prepared to meet future challenges.

In conclusion, the extended prospects and recommendations for the UAE's defence Emiratisation efforts highlight the importance of strengthening research and development, fostering collaboration and cooperation, investing in human resources development, exploring export opportunities, expanding the defence industrial base, and strategically planning for the long term. By implementing these measures, the UAE can continue its trajectory as a leader in defence technology, enhance regional security, and achieve its vision of economic diversification.

References For Further Reading

Al-Anezi, K., & Thabit, H. (2018). The transformation of the UAE defense industry: The rise of Abu Dhabi. Middle East Policy, 25(3), 53–68.

Al, Clayton Thomas, et. 2020. "Arms Sales in the Middle East: Trends and Analytical Perspectives for U.S. Policy." https://sgp.fas.org/crs/mideast/R44984.pdf.

Al-Hajji, M., & Awan, H. M. (2020). Armament support and indigenous defense industry: A case of the United Arab Emirates. Journal of Asian Security and International Affairs, 7(1), 58-82.

Almazrouei, N., & Youngs, R., Eds.(2020). Future Trends in the GCC. Gulf Research Center.

Almazroui, K., & Jones, T. (2022). "The Evolution of the UAE Defence Industry: Landscape, Challenges, and Prospects." *Defence Studies*, 22(2), 234-255.

Al-Mershed, M. (2017). Defense Offsets and Military Capabilities Development: The Case of the United Arab Emirates. Journal of Defense Studies, 11(2), 49–72.

Almezaini, Khalid S, and Jean-Marc Rickli. 2016. *The Small Gulf States*. Taylor & Francis.

Almezaini, K.S. (2012). The UAE and Foreign Policy: Foreign Aid, Identities and Interests. Routledge.

Alshehhi, A., & Watanabe, C. (2020). Assessing the United Arab Emirates: Defense Industrial Capabilities and the Role of Foreign Partnerships. Military and Strategic Affairs, 12(3), 99–134.

Ayoob, Mohammed. 2012. "TheArabSpring: ItsGeostrategicSignificance." *Middle East Policy* 19 (3): 84–97. https://doi.org/10.1111/j.1475-4967.2012.00549.x.

Baabood, Abdulla. 2003. "Dynamics and Determinants of the GCC States' Foreign Policy, with Special Reference to the EU." *The Review of International Affairs* 3 (2): 254–82. https://doi.org/10.1080/1475355032000240702.

Barany, Zoltan. 2020. "Indigenous Defense Industries in the Gulf." Www.csis.org. April 24, 2020. https://www.csis.org/analysis/indigenous-defense-industries-gulf.

———. 2021a. *Armies of Arabia: Military Politics and Effectiveness in the Gulf.* New York, Ny Oxford University Press.

———. 2021b. *The Political Economy of Gulf Defense Establishments.* Cambridge University Press.

Barnes, J.E., & Al-Najjar, D. (2021). "Military Technology Acquisition in the Middle East: The Case of the UAE." *Journal of Defense Analytics and Logistics, 5(1), 77-92.

Bazzi, S. (2016). The Dubai defense loophole: Arms smuggling via Dubai in the civil war in Libya. Security Studies, 25(4), 712–747.

Béraud-Sudreau, Lucie. 2020. *French Arms Exports.* Routledge.

Borchert, Heiko. 2018. "The Arab Gulf Defense Pivot: Defense Industrial Policy in a Changing Geostrategic Context." *Comparative Strategy* 37 (4): 299–315. https://doi.org/10.1080/01495933.2018.1497345.

Brookes, P., & Mohan, G. (2017). Defense reforms in the United Arab Emirates: The afterglow of the Arab Spring. Middle East Policy, 24(1), 34–47.

Buzan, B., & Wæver, O. (2010). Macrosecuritization and security constellations: Reconsidering scale in securitization theory. Review of International Studies, 36(2), 253-276.

Çağlar Kurç, Richard A Bitzinger, and Stephanie G Neuman. 2021. *Defence Industries in the 21st Century.* Routledge.

Cordesman, Anthony H, and Khalid R Al-Rodhan. 2006. *Gulf Military Forces in an Era of Asymmetric Wars.* Greenwood Publishing Group.

Davidson, C.M. (2009). *Abu Dhabi: Oil and Beyond*. Hurst.

DiGiovanna, Sean M, and Ann Markusen. 2003. *From Defense to Development?* Routledge.

Drwiega, Andrew. 2023. "Gulf Defence Industry Moves into High Gear." Asian Military Review. May 17, 2023. https://www.asianmilitaryreview.com/2023/05/gulf-defence-industry-moves-into-high-gear/.

Haroon Sheikh et al. n.d. "The Emerging GCC Defence Market." Accessed February 21, 2024. https://www.strategyand.pwc.com/m1/en/reports/the-emerging-gcc-defence-market.pdf.

Fetzek, K. (2015). The United Arab Emirates' approach to solving its defense industrialization problem. Middle East Policy, 22(4), 108-121.

Finlinson, Katie C. 2022. "The United Arab Emirates as a Case Study in Assessing Over-The-Horizon Nuclear Proliferation." *Journal of Advanced Military Studies* 13 (1): 112–29. https://muse.jhu.edu/article/851422.

Gardiner, K., & Hussein, A. (2023). "Innovation in Gulf Military Affairs: A Look at the UAE's Defense Sector." *International Security Journal*, 37(3), 305-322.

Gaub,F.(2016).Military Integration within the Arab Gulf States.*Oxford University Press.

Gaub, Florence. 2017. *Guardians of the Arab State. When Militaries Intervene in Politics, from Iraq to Mauritania.* London: Hurst & Company.

Gaub, Florence, and Zoe Stanley-Lockman. 2017. "Defence Industries in Arab States: Players and Strategies Chaillot Papers." https://www.iss.europa.eu/sites/default/files/EUISSFiles/CP_141_Arab_Defence.pdf.

GlobalData Plc. 2023. "United Arab Emirates Defense Market Size and Trends, Budget Allocation, Regulations, Key Acquisitions, Competitive Landscape and Forecast, 2022-2027." Market Research Reports & Consulting | GlobalData UK Ltd. March 6, 2023. https://www.globaldata.com/store/report/uae-defense-market-analysis/.

GlobalData's Intelligence Center. 2023. "United Arab Emirates (UAE) Defense Market Size and Trends, Budget Allocation, Regulations, Key Acquisitions, Competitive Landscape and Forecast, 2023-2028." Www.marketresearch.com. February 2023. https://www.marketresearch.com/GlobalData-v3648/United-Arab-Emirates-UAE-Defense-33621013/.

Grant, Jim, Fatema Shabbir Golawala, and Donelda S. McKechnie. 2007. "The United Arab Emirates: The Twenty-First Century Beckons." *Thunderbird International Business Review* 49 (4): 507–33. https://doi.org/10.1002/tie.20155.

GUERAICHE, WILLIAM, and Kristian Alexander. 2022. *Facets of Security in the United Arab Emirates.* Routledge.

Hellyer, P.H.A.R.I.T.H.P., & Karasik T.W., Eds.(2021).* The Emirates Through The Ages: An Economy Based On Knowledge And Sophistication Instead Of Oil". Springer.

Helou, Agnes. 2019. "Limits on Western Arms Exports Helped Spur Indigenous Saudi and UAE Defense Industry." Defense News. July 22, 2019. https://www.defensenews.com/global/mideast-africa/2019/07/22/limits-on-western-arms-exports-helped-spur-indigenous-saudi-and-uae-defense-industry/.

Hewitt, Daniel P. 1991. "Military Expenditure: International Comparison of Trends." *IMF Working Papers* 91 (54): i. https://doi.org/10.5089/9781451847420.001.

Hill, John. 2023. "UAE Implements Two-Pronged Plan to Expand and Modernise." Army Technology. February 14, 2023. https://www.army-technology.com/news/uae-defence-investment/.

Hoyt, Timothy D. 2017. *Military Industry and Regional Defense Policy.* Routledge.

Jawad, Haifaa A. 2016. *The Middle East in the New World Order.* Springer.

Kanwal, Gurmeet, Neha Kohli, and Institute For. 2018. *Defence Reforms: A National Imperative.* New Delhi: Institute For Defence Studies And Analyses.

Khalid Al-Jaber, and Dania Thafer. 2019. *The Dilemma of Security and Defense in the Gulf Region.* ISD LLC.

Kinninmont J.Eddie.(2016). After The Sheiks: The Coming Collapse Of Gulf Monarchs.Faber&Faber

Koch,C.T(2005)."The Politics role in changing defence Strategies.in GCC Countries. Lexington Books.

McGlinchey, S., Quelch, A., Rizk, N., & Simpson, A. (2018). The impact of the Arab Gulf states' defense expenditures on the U.S. economy. International Journal of Conflict Management, 29(3), 417–442.

Mezher, T., El-Sayed Mahmoud, A., & Fathallah Rachedi., K. (2022). "Energy Security and Defence Strategies in the Arabian Peninsula: Insights from UAE's Policy Shift." *Energy Policy*, 154(111964).

Partrick.N.D(2014)."Nationailism In The Gulf State."[Cambridge University Press]

Peterson, J.E. (2006). Defence and Security in the Arabian Peninsula. Gower Publishing Ltd.

Pradhan R.K., Singh S.K., Al Hammadi F.A.Y. (2021). "Defense Industrial Base Expansion in Middle Eastern Countries: A Study of Capacities Building Approach in Saudi Arabia and United Arab Emirates." *World Defence Systems Journal,* Vol XXIV Issue II.

Roberts, D.B. (2017). The UAE: Internal Dynamics and Foreign Policy. Columbia University Press.

Saab, Bilal Y., and Atlantic Council of the United States. 2014. *The Gulf Rising: Defense Industrialization in Saudi Arabia and the UAE.*

Salama, S.M,(2022). Security, Diplomacy And The Quest For Leadership In Defence Manufacturing Pursuits In Mena: Palgrave Macmillan.

Salehian, S., & Abdullaev I.N. (2020). "Foreign Arms Procurement in GCC Countries: Diversification Strategies with a Focus on the UAE." *Defence and Peace Economics*, 31(7), 755-771.

Schoeni, D., & Fuhrer, N. (2014). Regional Security Complex Theory (RSCT) applied: The Gulf Security Complex and the Question of Territoriality. Swiss Political Science Review, 20(2), 306–328.

Singh, Ravinder Pal. 1998. *Arms Procurement Decision Making: China, India, Israel, Japan, South Korea and Thailand.* Stockholm International Peace Research Institute.

Slijpe, Frank. (September 2017)."Under the radar. The United Arab Emirates, arms transfers and regional conflict." PAX. https://paxforpeace.nl/media/download/pax-report-under-the-radar--arms-trade.pdf

Soubrier, Emma. 2016. "Mirages of Power?" In *Gerlach Press eBooks,* 135–51. https://doi.org/10.2307/j.ctt1hj9wn0.11.

Thomas K.P., Madapallimattam B.A.J.(2022). "Public-private Partnerships in National Defense: Lessons from Abu Dhabi Ship Building." *Naval Engineering Journal,* Vol XXV No III.

Ulrichsen, K.C. (2017). *The United Arab Emirates: Power, Politics and Policy-Making*. Routledge.

United Arab Emirates - Country Commercial Guide. Defense.25-11-2023. https://www.trade.gov/country-commercial-guides/united-arab-emirates-defense

Vogt, Natalie, Adu-Boateng, Cyber Warfare Operations In GCC Defence Territories.Development and Implementation Insights.Praeger Security International.

Gulf دانيا ظافر. 2019. معضلة الأمن والدفاع في منطقة الخليج and, خالد الجابر International Forum.

Louth, John, Pierre Bontems, Bouchra Carlier, and Axel Pilottin. 2013. "OCCASIONAL PAPER DEFENCE INDUSTRY and the REINVIGORATED UK-UAE SECURITY RELATIONSHIP." https://static.rusi.org/201306_op_defence_industry_and_uk-uae.pdf.

Makara, Michael. 2013. "Coup-Proofing, Military Defection, and the Arab Spring." *Democracy and Security* 9 (4): 334–59. https://doi.org/10.1080/17419166.2013.802983.

McNeil, Harry. 2024. "UAE Defense Market Report Archives." Airforce Technology. 2024. https://www.airforce-technology.com/sector/uae-defense-market-report/.

Official Website of the International Trade Administration. 2020. "UAE Defense Sector Opportunities." Www.trade.gov. February 25, 2020. https://www.trade.gov/market-intelligence/uae-defense-sector-opportunities.

Roberts, David B. 2023. *Security Politics in the Gulf Monarchies*. Columbia University Press.

Saab, Bilal Y, and Atlantic Council Of The United States. 2014. *The Gulf Rising: Defense Industrialization in Saudi Arabia and the UAE*. Washington, DC: Atlantic Council.

Samaan, Jean-Loup. 2023. *New Military Strategies in the Gulf*. Bloomsbury Publishing.

Sandler, Todd, and Keith Hartley. 2007. *Handbook of Defense Economics*. Amsterdam: Elsevier North Holland; Oxford.

Sharif, Walid I. 2023. *Oil and Development in the Arab Gulf States*. Taylor & Francis.

Shubbar, Hashim. 2023. "The Political Economy of the United Arab Emirates Defence Industry | Al-Bayan Center." Al-Bayan Center for Planning and Studies. June 5, 2023. https://www.bayancenter.org/en/2023/06/3891/.

Sorenson, David S. 2023. *Civil-Military Relations in the Modern Middle East*. Rowman & Littlefield.

Suwaidi, Abdulla al-. 2011. "The United Arab Emirates at 40: A Balance Sheet." *Middle East Policy* 18 (4): 44–58. https://doi.org/10.1111/j.1475-4967.2011.00509.x.

Tactical Report, ed. 2024. "UAE Defense Industry: Missiles & Weapons (Projects and Exports)." Tactical Report. February 14, 2024. https://www.tacticalreport.com/in-depth/62530-uae-defense-industry-missiles-weapons-projects-and-exports.

Thafer, Dania. 2023. *Creative Insecurity*. Hurst Publishers.

Thornton, Rod, and Marina Miron. 2020. "Towards the 'Third Revolution in Military Affairs.'" *The RUSI Journal* 165 (3): 12–21. https://doi.org/10.1080/03071847.2020.1765514.

Ulrichsen, Kristian Coates. 2009. "Internal and External Security in the Arab Gulf States." *Middle East Policy* 16 (2): 39–58. https://doi.org/10.1111/j.1475-4967.2009.00390.x.

Vidal Ribe, Albert. 2023. "UAE Eyes Regional Edge on Arms Exports." IISS. November 14, 2023. https://www.iiss.org/online-analysis/military-balance/2023/11/uae-eyes-regional-edge-on-arms-exports/.

Y. Saab, Bilal. 2014. "The Gulf Rising: Defense Industrialization in Saudi Arabia and the UAE." Atlantic Council. May 7, 2014. https://www.atlanticcouncil.org/in-depth-research-reports/report/the-gulf-rising-defense-industrialization-in-saudi-arabia-and-the-uae/.

Yates, Athol. 2020. *The Evolution of the Armed Forces of the United Arab Emirates*. Warwick: Helion & Company Limited.

Yom, Sean L., and F. Gregory Gause. 2012. "Resilient Royals: How Arab Monarchies Hang On." *Journal of Democracy* 23 (4): 74–88. https://doi.org/10.1353/jod.2012.0062.

Young, Karen E. 2017. "A New Politics of GCC Economic Statecraft: The Case of UAE Aid and Financial Intervention in Egypt." *Journal of Arabian Studies* 7 (1): 113–36. https://doi.org/10.1080/21534764.2017.1316051.